Dog Lover's
Wordsearch

Dog Lover's
Wordsearch

More than 100 themed puzzles about our canine companions

This edition published in 2022 by Arcturus Publishing Limited
26/27 Bickels Yard, 151–153 Bermondsey Street,
London SE1 3HA

AD010154NT

Printed in the UK

```
W Y A T B L O O D H O U N D R
R L N A I N A R E M O P N E E
S E I O K M E O A S B I A K T
H A L K B H P B L P H M M R N
E T G I P B R T S D A O R E I
T A E E I R S Z L A R E P O L
L P H R T W P F I S R E B P P
A S A T V R T N V G I D O I K
N T A P I U O T O U R R D H E
D N O N I I R N O W J O I C E
Y K G V S L E E H R Y B C S S
A E P O O D L E N S K J W Y H
R B J S L B R O D A R B A L O
Y T C O S S C H N A U Z E R N
A G G C A T T L E D O G C D D
```

◊ AUSTRALIAN CATTLE DOG

◊ BELGIAN MALINOIS

◊ BELGIAN TERVUREN

◊ BLOODHOUND

◊ BORDER COLLIE

◊ BRITTANY

◊ DOBERMAN PINSCHER

◊ ENGLISH SPRINGER SPANIEL

◊ GERMAN SHEPHERD

◊ GERMAN SHORTHAIRED POINTER

◊ GOLDEN RETRIEVER

◊ IRISH WATER SPANIEL

◊ KEESHOND

◊ LABRADOR

◊ MINIATURE SCHNAUZER

◊ PAPILLON

◊ PEMBROKE WELSH CORGI

◊ POMERANIAN

◊ POODLE

◊ ROTTWEILER

◊ SCHIPPERKE

◊ SHETLAND SHEEPDOG

◊ VIZSLA

Terrific Terriers

```
S E L A D R E T T A P T B D M
E H S I T T O C S L I I N I T
A B W K M L L A B B L A U S M
L E E E E Y K S E H L U I I A
Y D L R S Y P T N E S R B N U
H L A R O T A Y K N E I H Y S
A I D Y B N H A K T J S R N T
M N E B O A L I S S L W R I R
H G R L S W K E G E E I E C A
C T I U T L H R W H A C J I L
I O A E O C O X E C L S E M I
W N R F N H J O T D E A E M A
R E R A E A D F Y M R K N L N
O O M I E R I H S K R O Y D E
N J A C K R U S S E L L B I A
```

◊ AIREDALE

◊ AUSTRALIAN

◊ BEDLINGTON

◊ BORDER

◊ BOSTON

◊ BULL

◊ CAIRN

◊ CESKY

◊ FOX

◊ IRISH

◊ JACK RUSSELL

◊ KERRY BLUE

◊ LAKELAND

◊ MANCHESTER

◊ NORFOLK

◊ NORWICH

◊ PATTERDALE

◊ SCOTTISH

◊ SEALYHAM

◊ SKYE

◊ TIBETAN

◊ WELSH

◊ WEST
  HIGHLAND

◊ YORKSHIRE

```
H S I L G N E S T Y H A P P Y
S M A L L E S T A D A E H U L
E A C E S E Y T I L I G A R E
I L Q R J W S R H O M E I S V
S D U E U T C A P M O C N U I
F E I C R E B M U N F N D I T
R S R T H B Y S C S F E I T A
I C E I N A W A L K S I C S L
E R D W U E N Y D Y P D A O E
N I I E D Q M N R T R E T O R
D B S N N A E T E E I B I D E
L E T L U S E R R L N O V E V
Y D U B O S T O N A G W E X E
V E O B R I G H T B P U O U L
Y H T L A E H E R U T A N T C
```

Group: Non-sporting/Utility

Background: The <u>smallest</u> of the bull-type breeds, the <u>Boston</u> terrier was the <u>result</u> of breeding <u>between</u> a bulldog and an <u>English</u> terrier. The <u>owner</u> of Judge—the resulting <u>offspring</u>—took his <u>new</u> dog <u>home</u> to Boston where he <u>acquired</u> his name.

Description: This <u>compact</u> breed has a <u>relatively</u> square <u>head</u> with <u>erect</u> ears and usually a distinctive "<u>tuxedo</u>" patterned coat in a <u>number</u> of shades. It has <u>round</u> and alert eyes <u>indicative</u> of its intelligent <u>nature</u>.

Temperament: The Boston terrier is <u>described</u> as a <u>bright</u>, lively, <u>clever</u>, and determined breed. This makes for a <u>smart</u> and <u>friendly</u> dog that can <u>channel</u> its intelligence into <u>agility</u> and <u>obedience</u> <u>pursuits</u>.

Energy Level: Though <u>happy</u> in an <u>apartment</u> home with small <u>outside</u> space this breed <u>requires</u> one or two <u>walks</u> per <u>day</u> to <u>stay</u> fit and <u>healthy</u>.

```
J E H B E A G L E F C B O F I
P Y K C A B E G D I R O P I J
R N A R D N U O H Y E R G N N
A A W R A M F T T L B Z W Y E
I H A S E G F U M E E O F V S
H G Z J K I Y O W H S I R I A
G F A V K N R L X T R S T I B
U A B U A T T R O H L I A A E
O T L Z T D I G A P O F R B O
L A I O N C O O N H O U N D G
S B L L B L O O D H O U N D N
I P H R E S H O A R A H P D E
Z T I P S W H T E P P I H W D
G I S D N U H S H C A D H H O
T W D N U O H R E E D T O W P
```

- ◊ AFGHAN HOUND
- ◊ AZAWAKH
- ◊ BASENJI
- ◊ BASSET HOUND
- ◊ BEAGLE
- ◊ BLOODHOUND
- ◊ BORZOI
- ◊ COONHOUND
- ◊ DACHSHUND
- ◊ DEERHOUND
- ◊ FINNISH SPITZ
- ◊ FOXHOUND
- ◊ GREYHOUND
- ◊ HARRIER
- ◊ IBIZAN HOUND
- ◊ IRISH WOLFHOUND
- ◊ PHARAOH HOUND
- ◊ PLOTT HOUND
- ◊ POLYGAR HOUND
- ◊ PORTUGUESE PODENGO
- ◊ RHODESIAN RIDGEBACK
- ◊ SALUKI
- ◊ SLOUGHI
- ◊ WHIPPET

Dogs in Fiction – Part One

```
L K E J U B A P F L O R K D S
A C D B U L L S E Y E T R N E
S O O H A C P I L O T O O U L
K T P S W P E A B H F B P T K
A E S U P E G T R F P R D K C
J I A L I R L N I U E T A P I
E A G F J D V L A N U M O R P
N R E H N I C C I F L U F F Y
P G R T N T R O J N E S T A D
Y O L R K A J F O R G T A N I
T S B D M N D V B E I T I S K
K O N U H L I D T L N B O H T
J N P O C T U U L J A Y S N W
U O J S W K C U J O N B A Y F
Y B V L C Y P A T R A S C H E
```

◊ ARGOS

◊ BUCK

◊ BULL'S-EYE

◊ CLIFFORD

◊ CUJO

◊ FLUFFY

◊ FLUSH

◊ GASPODE

◊ JOHN JOINER

◊ LASKA

◊ LASSIE

◊ NANA

◊ OLD DAN

◊ PATRASCHE

◊ PERDITA

◊ PICKLES

◊ PILOT

◊ RIBSY

◊ SNOWY

◊ SPOT

◊ TOCK

◊ TOTO

◊ WELLINGTON

◊ WHITE FANG

```
P P B T D K R L A Q E K B Q B
B E X G A B Y X E P R A K Y E
R Y H X B E F A F H P Y I U N
E T I S N J B D K V U O L S D
T R O K I H C A H A N L L A A
A A H U S O Z I R G B Q I L L
G K M V V T N F O R V A A T O
N R E L N L A O F X Y N N Y C
E E D A J A A T I I I N A G H
Y N N I G B C E O H N Y N X I
M A X K J X C J C W D N O V N
B T O A N I U A S D D S C B O
O X J O M P L Q U C T C C D O
K E I L L I A B M H G Q B J K
U A T A D I Z O B M O K M Y S
```

◊ APPOLLO   ◊ ENDAL   ◊ LA CHINA

◊ BAILLIE   ◊ FINN   ◊ LAIKA

◊ BALTO   ◊ GINNY   ◊ LUCCA

◊ BARRY   ◊ HACHIKO   ◊ MKOMBOZI

◊ BRETAGNE   ◊ JADE   ◊ SALTY

◊ BUDDY   ◊ JET OF IADA   ◊ SHEP

◊ CHINOOK   ◊ KABANG   ◊ SINBAD

◊ CONAN   ◊ KILLIAN   ◊ TRAKR

```
K H U C K Y C S P M R E G O R
E R W W T J J W Y J O C F S D
P F A R N C D D L W H A M S J
U A I B V V T U L C T R P E W
R D T B L I G S O G N O P C E
O U V C B U R G R S T H C N I
V I T B H D C C A T U A R I T
E S S K G V A K Y A P D U R T
R E P S A J G N Y T S U E P O
E S E Y P S N H A I A C L U C
G F R N H A W I E N V H L R S
E V D N N E N I N A K E A A H
N D I E P F G C F W G S E M A
T J T P G G D A N N Y S J A C
S O A T L O B R E D N U H T E
```

◊ ANITA

◊ CAPTAIN

◊ CRUELLA DE VIL

◊ DANNY

◊ DIRTY DAWSON

◊ DUCHESS

◊ HORACE BADDUN

◊ JASPER BADDUN

◊ KANINE KRUNCHIES

◊ LUCKY

◊ NANNY

◊ PATCH

◊ PENNY

◊ PERDITA

◊ PONGO

◊ PRINCESS

◊ REGENT'S PARK

◊ ROGER

◊ ROLLY

◊ ROVER

◊ SCOTTIE

◊ SERGEANT TIBBS

◊ SPOTTY

◊ THUNDERBOLT

◊ TWILIGHT BARK

Excerpt from *The Call of the Wild* by Jack London

Buck was neither house-dog nor kennel-dog. The whole realm was his. He plunged into the swimming tank or went hunting with the Judge's sons; he escorted Mollie and Alice, the Judge's daughters, on long twilight or early morning rambles; on wintry nights he lay at the Judge's feet before the roaring library fire; he carried the Judge's grandsons on his back, or rolled them in the grass, and guarded their footsteps through wild adventures down to the fountain in the stable yard, and even beyond, where the paddocks were, and the berry patches. Among the terriers he stalked imperiously, and Toots and Ysabel he utterly ignored, for he was king,— king over all creeping, crawling, flying things of Judge Miller's place, humans included.

```
I M A D V E N T U R E S I E P
P I C R A W L I N G O M A E L
A L D K B U C K D N P R L F U
T L A E N A G E S E L B B T N
C E Y C L I K H R Y A T E E G
H R L I E L A I T T F O Y R E
E S C O A J O T S E H O O R D
S E G T H U D R N Y R T N I W
N S S N S W E O J U W S D E Y
A E A L I B R A R Y O T A R F
M G Y R L K O R O N E F R S L
U D B R G E N I U T T E R L Y
H U N T I N G N L E B A S Y I
U J K N A T I G M O L L I E N
M L A E R U H S E L B M A R G
```

13

Popular Breed Profile: Cavalier King Charles Spaniel

```
Y H C R A N O M L E I N A P S
N S J F R I E N D L Y M Y S E
A E U G E S F L U M I R Y T U
M L T N H P G F L E U O I N R
D R P O T A E E H T U H E A O
E A A L O C L N N T W R E I P
T H D C A E E E D T D L C R E
P C A R T L C O A L L S N A A
E B G C B I O E I S T E E V N
C L K S S R V H K R T D N A H
C A I I S N C E U H L A I L O
A C L N N E K O A T L R M K U
E K E T K G C P N G A K O C S
Y B U R O E P C F O M N R A E
D E E R B Y D P A H S L P B J
```

Group: Toy

Background: Toy spaniel breeds have been closely linked with European monarchy as far back as the 16th century, coming to prominence in the courts of King Charles I and his son Charles II.

Description: The accepted coat variants are black and tan, black and white, ruby, and Blenheim. They are a reasonably small breed with a long silky coat, long ears, and dark eyes.

Temperament: Friendly, affectionate, and graceful, this gentle breed will adapt to many environments and is happy around other dogs and children.

Energy Level: A moderately active dog, this breed is happy in a medium-sized house as long as there is access to at least a small outdoor space.

```
Y N O S N H O J F M F B O E S
P E B E A F S Y I O F H M N M
I M N R P L L E W O C A N G
I O W T A P C R Y G C V T M D
V O D T R U C Y D G E H Y N M
D L E E O A O L R S W A N K A
R B N C I B C A A O W L V S L
A T O O A R N C H R C I I K E
W R J M R D F I M O K A C E X
D A A L E Y K Y O P V S T S A
E W L S I V B P E R I C O C N
U E I R E Y E D E S I Y R N D
B T B C K R D G R S C Y I O E
Y S D D E C E T K O G S A I R
L K C J T T T D N A L L O H E
```

◊ <u>ALEXANDER</u>
<u>THE GREAT</u>

◊ AMANDA
<u>SEYFRIED</u>

◊ ARIANA
<u>GRANDE</u>

◊ BARACK
<u>OBAMA</u>

◊ BRADLEY
<u>COOPER</u>

◊ CHRIS <u>EVANS</u>

◊ DWAYNE
<u>JOHNSON</u>

◊ <u>EDWARD VII</u>

◊ HILARY <u>SWANK</u>

◊ <u>ICE T</u>

◊ JENNY <u>SLATE</u>

◊ JON <u>HAMM</u>

◊ KALEY <u>CUOCO</u>

◊ KELLY
<u>CLARKSON</u>

◊ KRISTEN <u>BELL</u>

◊ <u>LORD BYRON</u>

◊ ORLANDO
<u>BLOOM</u>

◊ PAUL
<u>MCCARTNEY</u>

◊ QUEEN
<u>VICTORIA</u>

◊ RICKY <u>GERVAIS</u>

◊ ROD <u>STEWART</u>

◊ SIMON <u>COWELL</u>

◊ TOM <u>HARDY</u>

◊ TOM <u>HOLLAND</u>

```
L O N G T R I P E D R P P R W
S W O H S E C D F E L A G G S
L O V K E Y I X A T C R B S N
D R N S H G N S M N O T K J E
N E J E G H N W S I G Y S G T
E T G R E O K E G A L E A B T
I A M K W Y D O L P L R R F I
R W B N U S E H T L U R O Y K
F Y W M K X X S C O A R Z B J
W A E L A P F A C T E H L P Z
Y R Z H H G L E N S A O C E E
Z O I I O O I E T U W W N L C
P O R L C M E C I U R E S T B
V H P L X J E U P R O B L E M
Y E N S K A T E B O A R D E L
```

◊ *CHALLENGE TO LASSIE*

◊ *COURAGE OF LASSIE*

◊ *DANGEROUS PARTY*

◊ *DIGGING UP DANGER*

◊ *FOREST RANGER HANDBOOK*

◊ *HILLS OF HOME*

◊ *HOORAY FOR LASSIE!*

◊ *LASSIE AND THE KITTENS*

◊ *LASSIE COME HOME*

◊ *LASSIE FINDS A FRIEND*

◊ *LASSIE SHOWS THE WAY*

◊ *LASSIE: OLD ONE EYE*

◊ *LASSIE: THE PRIZE*

◊ *LASSIE'S LONG TRIP*

◊ *SKATEBOARD DARE*

◊ *THE BIG BLOWUP*

◊ *THE MAGIC OF LASSIE*

◊ *THE PAINTED HILLS*

◊ *THE PUPPY PROBLEM*

◊ *THE SUN COMES UP*

◊ *WATER WATCHDOG*

```
B D N A L D N U O F W E N B D
B U R A E L U T E D N O T O C
E L H A S A A P S O H D E L D
R E T T E S L B U R E E G O I
G K I M N S V P D L I D O G E
A D P N R T E N V L I R D N U
M R Y K E O O G L W E A P E A
A A R N B H D O N E I E E S D
S I E Y S G C N F I H B E E N
C R N E W L A W O Y K H H B A
O B E G C C F O O M S E S J L
N K E T H Y G E Y L O K P H T
D A S I A A H W L F O K Y P E
J L N H A V A N E S E W L E H
J A O H S E N U Z T H I H S S
```

◊ AFGHAN HOUND

◊ BEARDED COLLIE

◊ BERGAMASCO

◊ BERNESE MOUNTAIN DOG

◊ BOLOGNESE

◊ BRIARD

◊ COTON DE TULEAR

◊ ENGLISH SETTER

◊ GREAT PYRENEES

◊ HAVANESE

◊ JAPANESE CHIN

◊ KEESHOND

◊ KOMONDOR

◊ LHASA APSO

◊ LOWCHEN

◊ NEWFOUND-LAND

◊ OLD ENGLISH SHEEPDOG

◊ PEKINGESE

◊ PULI

◊ ROUGH COLLIE

◊ SHETLAND SHEEPDOG

◊ SHIH TZU

◊ SKYE TERRIER

Dogs That Need Big Homes – Part One

- ◊ AKITA
- ◊ ALASKAN MALAMUTE
- ◊ AZAWAKH
- ◊ BASSET HOUND
- ◊ BEARDED COLLIE
- ◊ BORZOI
- ◊ BRACCO ITALIAN
- ◊ BRIAR
- ◊ CANAAN DOG

- ◊ CLUMBER SPANIEL
- ◊ DEERHOUND
- ◊ FOXHOUND
- ◊ GERMAN SHEPHERD
- ◊ GIANT SCHNAUZER
- ◊ GREAT DANE
- ◊ GREENLAND DOG
- ◊ HOVAWART

- ◊ IRISH WOLFHOUND
- ◊ MAREMMA SHEEPDOG
- ◊ PYRENEAN MASTIFF
- ◊ ROTTWEILER
- ◊ SAINT BERNARD
- ◊ SIBERIAN HUSKY
- ◊ STANDARD POODLE

```
F E M O C E B C O M M O N L Y
G N E M A N A M I A B L E A A
N E P D N U O H E O M P R C R
I M U E C O E F T E U N W I A
W R R B I S I T N R S H E S L
A A P B E L E T S H A G G Y U
L W O E N R A U A P O U R H G
T N S W T L I E P L Y O A P E
U H E S M T R L R H U R L R R
O O U D B A I E U H F M D M A
B M O R R E T N L O O K I N G
R E E O D A T V P K C I H T N
E E N W W I G R E Q U I R E S
D Y L G N I S I R P R U S N U
F C U G O D E V E L O P E D J
```

Group: Hound

Background: An <u>ancient</u> breed that, <u>unsurprisingly</u> given its <u>name</u>, was <u>developed</u> for the <u>hunting</u> of <u>otter</u>. With the <u>outlawing</u> of this <u>pursuit</u> the breed has <u>become</u> increasingly <u>rare</u>.

Description: Bred for <u>life</u> in the <u>water</u>, this rather <u>shaggy</u> <u>looking</u> <u>large</u> breed has <u>webbed</u> feet and a <u>thick</u> double-layered <u>rough</u> coat to keep it <u>warm</u> and <u>dry</u>.

Temperament: The <u>words</u> most <u>commonly</u> <u>applied</u> to this <u>breed</u> are even-tempered and <u>amiable</u>.

Energy Level: As a <u>hound</u> that was <u>bred</u> with a <u>purpose</u> this breed <u>requires</u> <u>regular</u> <u>physical</u> and <u>mental</u> <u>stimulation</u>. A <u>large</u> <u>home</u> and <u>garden</u> are a <u>must</u>.

Mrs. Darling <u>loved</u> to have everything just so, and Mr. <u>Darling</u> had a <u>passion</u> for being exactly like his neighbours; so, of course, they had a <u>nurse</u>. As they were poor, owing to the <u>amount</u> of milk the <u>children</u> drank, this nurse was a prim Newfoundland dog, called <u>Nana</u>, who had belonged to no one in <u>particular</u> until the Darlings <u>engaged</u> her. She had always thought children important, <u>however</u>, and the Darlings had <u>become</u> acquainted with her in <u>Kensington</u> Gardens, where she <u>spent</u> most of her spare time <u>peeping</u> into perambulators, and was much <u>hated</u> by careless nursemaids, <u>whom</u> she followed to their <u>homes</u> and complained of to their mistresses. She proved to be quite a <u>treasure</u> of a nurse. How thorough she was at <u>bath-time</u>, and up at any moment of the night if one of her charges made the <u>slightest</u> cry. Of course her <u>kennel</u> was in the nursery. She had a <u>genius</u> for knowing when a <u>cough</u> is a thing to have no <u>patience</u> with and when it needs <u>stocking</u> around your <u>throat</u>. She believed to her last day in old-fashioned <u>remedies</u> like rhubarb <u>leaf</u>, and made sounds of <u>contempt</u> <u>over</u> all this new-fangled talk about <u>germs</u>, and so on. It was a <u>lesson</u> in propriety to see her escorting the children to <u>school</u>, walking sedately by their <u>side</u> when they were well <u>behaved</u>, and <u>butting</u> them back into line if they <u>strayed</u>.

```
T P M E T N O C D E Y A R T S
R S L P A R T I C U L A R H H
E L E M I T H T A B C E S R O
C D O T B E C O M E A D C O W
N G E V H G E R M S T E H A E
I I E S A D I R E G S A O A E
T K E P N H E L E N P H L M R
A C P E A K E N S I N G T O N
P O I N N C I B L O V E R U O
M T N T O U L E S S O N L N I
O S G U S D A R L I N G S T S
H E G N R F S G N I T T U B S
W H E D I S E I D E M E R L A
C H I L D R E N G A G E D D P
```

```
G R E Y H O U N D W V N P H H
E R E Z U A N H C S A E G O O
I I F N L D E E R H O U N D A
T F L S A B G A G E O C B R R
P D I L C R L F N G N P A M A
R G R B O S A A S U E T M E H
H U I E Z C D M N A T R P D P
O A S I H T R A I E L O M R E
D F V S A P I E R E O U L A A
E J L E E T E R D D W E K V N
S J R H A L I H L R S S A I M
I G L M U E L E S I O Z R O B
A J L Y R S N A M R E B O D G
N A Z I B I K A R I S T E T G
D D N V E G S Y T E P P I H W
```

◊ AFGHAN HOUND

◊ AUSTRALIAN SHEPHERD

◊ BORDER COLLIE

◊ BORZOI

◊ DALMATIAN

◊ DOBERMAN PINSCHER

◊ GERMAN SHEPHERD

◊ GIANT SCHNAUZER

◊ GREAT DANE

◊ GREYHOUND

◊ IBIZAN HOUND

◊ JACK RUSSELL

◊ PHARAOH HOUND

◊ RAT TERRIER

◊ RHODESIAN RIDGEBACK

◊ SALUKI

◊ SCOTTISH DEERHOUND

◊ SIBERIAN HUSKY

◊ STANDARD POODLE

◊ VIZSLA

◊ WEIMARANER

◊ WHIPPET

```
N R E H T U O S S P S K T M I
P E L N P O V U K M H J C V D
E M M A N S S E C D S A H A T
Y I C M A S U J N L P Y L M E
A L K L O F R O N A N B D L B
F H I L A D C U I A O U T U S
C S O I R U S S I A N O L C K
H M I H O W L T S P B L V H T
I T O T N E I H E L D P B I U
E N W K Y H A N A O B Y E R R
N U E R A H I T G R S G L I N
G A K T U P O N A B U C G B S
R L K S L I S Q P I A C I A P
I A N A S E U Q R A M Y A Y I
S L D H V E F U E G I A N A T
```

◊ ALAUNT

◊ ALPINE MASTIFF

◊ BELGIAN MASTIFF

◊ BRAQUE DUPUY

◊ CHIEN-GRIS

◊ CHIRIBAYA DOG

◊ DALBO DOG

◊ DOGO CUBANO

◊ FUEGIAN DOG

◊ HALLS HEELER

◊ HARE INDIAN DOG

◊ LIMER

◊ MARQUESAN DOG

◊ MOLOSSUS

◊ NORFOLK SPANIEL

◊ PAISLEY TERRIER

◊ RUSSIAN TRACKER

◊ SALISH WOOL DOG

◊ SOUTHERN HOUND

◊ TAHITIAN DOG

◊ TALBOT HOUND

◊ TOY BULLDOG

◊ TURNSPIT DOG

◊ WELSH HILLMAN

```
A C E T H E W O N D E R D O G
S N I G G I H I R B U D D Y O
Y F S A N G G U E N G M F H D
E S D Y R I J K N K A O N S E
D N S C G B N N R D I I R Y H
Y O M S O C N T I E T P R F T
L C C F A Y P S H N C U S O R
C B P P P P O U I G T C G R E
E V R P K N F T M E I A O M D
G S I I S U N L R U O L R S N
A K O E G I C R A Z O R L O U
S E K O R I Y Y N M S A K C H
D Y N A M I T E T H E D O G T
S K E I G G U T D A I S Y I R
R K A E R T S R E V L I S K M
```

◊ ACE THE WONDER DOG

◊ BRIGITTE

◊ BUDDY

◊ CLYDE

◊ COSMO

◊ DAISY

◊ DARLA

◊ DYNAMITE THE DOG

◊ ENZO

◊ FLAME

◊ HIGGINS

◊ LIGHTNING

◊ MADISON

◊ MOOSE

◊ RIN TIN TIN

◊ SANGGUEN

◊ SILVER STREAK

◊ SKIPPY

◊ SOCCER

◊ SPIKE

◊ SYKES

◊ TERRY

◊ THUNDER THE DOG

◊ UGGIE

Dogs of Folklore and Myth

```
M N X Q U O G N A I T O G D S
A I T U U D I S N R K G G Q I
E M R R D J G P U U G W I F N
R I E S Q O K X R R Y O A P I
A R L H U G R I B L E U S L L
K G E A A S I M L E X B U U I
C H G R I N U G A M I I R S A
U C M R U J I R Q R S P A E F
H R Q C A V A L L O C B W H C
S U D L U V T A N E U H A K I
K H F J R U N E Q L U P R V O
C C W A E R A L G Q I Q I R N
A B H F F F S A J Y U J D M U
L S H M Z F E P O J E D A C K
B T J Y R G P S F R E Y B U G
```

◊ ARGOS	◊ FAILINIS	◊ LUISON
◊ BLACK SHUCK	◊ FREYBUG	◊ MAERA
◊ BUL-GAE	◊ GARMR	◊ OKURI-INU
◊ CADEJO	◊ GELERT	◊ PESANTA
◊ CAVALL	◊ GWYLLGI	◊ QIQIRN
◊ CERBERUS	◊ INUGAMI	◊ Q'URSHA
◊ CHURCH GRIM	◊ IRAWARU	◊ SHARVARA
◊ DORMARCH	◊ LAELAPS	◊ TIANGOU

Popular Breed Profile: Golden Retriever

```
E A S Y A F C P O P U L A R K
L E V E L K L S E R I U Q E R
I A I N T E L L I G E N T E S
W L L L A N I M A L S F C T E
T F I S B C E S G D A A R G R
C U E L B V O U E M P A O O V
B L I L I Y I N I S N D U L I
P N A T R D I L F G T G N D C
D C C E E A I C E I L S D E E
K A G C M E L R H O D G R N A
Y A V E S H S O S O E E O I T
E G R A L Y E S N J I S N A F
E T A T S E Y I U G U C O T L
H T U O M D E E W T E C E N A
H C U S L O H S I T T O C S T
```

Group: Sporting/Gundog

Background: They were first bred on the Scottish Guisachan estate by Lord Tweedmouth in the mid-1800s. A popular working dog, they are most closely associated with service roles, such as being guide dogs for the blind.

Description: A solidly built, medium-sized dog, named for its glossy golden coat which may be flat or wavy, with round, dark eyes and usually a black nose.

Temperament: An intelligent, trainable, confident, and friendly dog, it is easy to see why the golden retriever has remained one of the most popular choices of pet for families for decades. They are eager to please and tend to get along well with other animals, children, and strangers.

Energy Level: An extremely active dog that requires a high level of exercise, a large house, and outside space.

◇ BRINGING TOYS

◇ COMFORTING YOU

◇ CUDDLING

◇ EXCITED CIRCLING

◇ EYE CONTACT

◇ FOLLOWING

◇ JUMPING

◇ LEANING

◇ LICKING

◇ LOYALTY

◇ NOSING

◇ NUDGING

◇ PLAYING

◇ PLEASED YOU'RE HOME

◇ ROLLING

◇ SIGHING

◇ SLEEPING TOGETHER

◇ SMILING

◇ STEALING SOCKS

◇ WAGGING TAIL

◇ WRESTLING

Excerpt from *The History of Pompey the Little* by Francis Coventry

Pompey, the son of Julio and Phyllis, was born A.D. 1735, at Bologna in Italy, a place famous for lap-dogs and sausages. Both his parents were of the most illustrious families, descended from a long train of ancestors, who had figured in many parts of Europe, and lived in intimacy with the greatest men of the time.—They had frequented the chambers of the proudest beauties, and had access to the closets of the greatest princes. Cardinals, kings, popes, emperors, were all happy in their acquaintance: and I am told the elder branch of the family now lives with his present holiness, in the papal palace at Rome.

But Julio, the father of my hero, being a younger brother of a numerous family, fell to the share of an Italian nobleman at Bologna, who was about this time engaged in an intrigue with a celebrated courtezan of the place. And little Julio often attending him when he made his visits to her, as it is the nature of all servants to imitate the vices of their masters, he also commenced an affair of gallantry with a favourite… named Phyllis, at that time the darling of this *fille de joye*.

```
S E C N I R P S E I T U A E B
O R E H K P S I L L Y H P U Y
I N T I M A C Y N I N I A R T
O F N J T L I M I T A T E O Y
L G A N M A L S O T D S R P H
S R N M A C L I C L R S P E C
T E G I I E S Y V E H A O P N
N A O D L L E R B E H U M A A
E T L U E R I M O K S S P E R
R E O O A M A E I T G A E R B
A S B H N H A D S T S G Y U R
P T S K C H G N I D N E T T A
L A P A P R E H T A F S C A E
E Y O J U L I O D E G A G N E
R S U O R E M U N R I A F F A
```

```
B T R S K H Y T I L G G N B U
P U S C P L W A T A P A D D Y
C J I L L Y L N B E S C Y P Y
B M I I Y B A L T U R L J U M
F U W W E R E L I Z A B E T H
E I T R G D E V O N M I A M I
W G T T T J O R N I T S U J D
E O B H O Y K J P U S T O O B
I Y I S M N T N N O Y D C M R
S S H B M M S L O W K O R A G
S U I C Y K E D T P C F I I A
A Y W E N Z A M M E A B C S K
C C B A A N T E A S E I K I I
T J H H N C T I B L L O Y E N
L G I Y N J W N L E K E P T G
```

◊ ALBERT	◊ ELIZABETH	◊ KNOPA
◊ BELL	◊ EMMA	◊ MAISIE
◊ BOOTS	◊ GABLE	◊ MIAMI
◊ BRETT	◊ GRANT	◊ MICK
◊ BUTTONS	◊ HANK	◊ PADDY
◊ CASSIE	◊ HAZELNUT	◊ RICKY
◊ COCO	◊ JILLY	◊ TEASE
◊ DANNY	◊ JOSHUA	◊ TOMMY
◊ DEVON	◊ JUSTIN	◊ WILLY
◊ DYLAN	◊ KING	◊ YOGI

```
Y I J N E S A B T S A A O S T
O D A C H S H U N D O F T U B
R A S E L A D E R I A F L I I
K P V C E I L L O C U E S L O
S E A C H I N E S E A N U H N
H M R M R N M S U R H P Y N O
I A N R A E A O R C H I D O T
R L O H Y H D U J F S N Y F G
E T H G M B Y R Z M M S N F N
K E C A Y O L L O E O C O I I
A S I B I E C U A B R H R R L
V E B Y K S E C E E S E F G D
W I R E F O X K J J S R O E E
A D N U O H Y E R G W K L U B
I R I S H E L D O O P O K Y I
```

◊ AFFEN-
PINSCHER

◊ AIREDALE
TERRIER

◊ BASENJI

◊ BEARDED
COLLIE

◊ BEDLINGTON
TERRIER

◊ BICHON FRISE

◊ BORDER
TERRIER

◊ BRUSSELS
GRIFFON

◊ CESKY
TERRIER

◊ CHINESE
CRESTED

◊ COTON DE
TULEAR

◊ DACHSHUND

◊ GREYHOUND

◊ IRISH WATER
SPANIEL

◊ KERRY BLUE
TERRIER

◊ MALTESE

◊ MINIATURE
SCHNAUZER

◊ NORFOLK
TERRIER

◊ PERUVIAN INCA
ORCHID

◊ POODLE

◊ PULI

◊ SEALYHAM
TERRIER

◊ WIRE FOX
TERRIER

◊ YORKSHIRE
TERRIER

```
E R U T C I P R E G U L A R E
L U F T H G I L E D G N Y G O
B L A C K I T F I N E P R A S
E S U O H R W H I E P A H S M
B N B C A T O M D A L T S A A
I S U D R M R C H I N E S E L
R O E O E A D O L E Y C G U L
C R H L H H S A M E O N R S L
S S A C B H G T E T A O N U T
E N U E P O R U E R U K F A N
D C O M P A N I O N A R P L I
N W A F P U G E D R E U P L A
P O T A T O E S D E H B Q Y P
D E T I R I P S H P E T Y S G
R E H T O N A C S N O U T E D
```

Group: Toy

Background: Another dog that gained popularity through association with nobles, initially the Chinese emperors of its homeland. It was then taken to Europe by traders where it became a mascot for the House of Orange.

Description: A small and relatively square dog, with a large head and short, snouted face and large, round eyes. It has a fine, short coat that is most usually fawn or black.

Temperament: The words used to describe the pug paint a delightful picture of a charming, spirited, and lively companion.

Energy Level: Though happy to be couch potatoes they need regular exercise to stay in shape, but an apartment home is fine for this cheerful pet.

Dogs of the White House

```
Y T R E B I L A R A C V V G V
L U C C G N K L U C K Y V Y O
K C A J K C A L B A N C E N C
Y C J K J H R Y L N E R T N T
L J A J I A T A L A C G O U L
E Y S R K N F R E C K L E S N
I Y D D U B G E I L R A H C E
L W R E B S V T O I W P L Y E
L S G A S V O K I R E I F O B
I W P D A S H R J M M K P B E
M M R O P P P A S H A S W D P
V E S J T J M H H Y J H G L A
Y O R B O R D A R N O A O O G
V R A G B W J N H E R B M E K
D A S Y E N R A B C X I K U Y
```

◊ BARNEY	◊ FALA	◊ PASHA
◊ BLACKJACK	◊ FRECKLES	◊ REX
◊ BUDDY	◊ KING TIMAHOE	◊ ROB ROY
◊ CARUSO	◊ LIBERTY	◊ SKIP
◊ CHAMP	◊ LUCKY	◊ SPOT
◊ CHARLIE	◊ MAJOR	◊ SUNNY
◊ DASH	◊ MILLIE	◊ VETO
◊ EDGAR	◊ OLD BOY	◊ YUKI

```
X G D L O N E A R J Q J S Q H
P K G I O P T S D N O V M W K
M Y U O L A X Y A C S N C W H
S X O U D N U I K H A S T R O
L M T R R R R G D E C E E X A
I O N L E B E E I V T K D K J
O L U Y T Z B D D E I E A B K
N E R F S O O A N P P M U Q K
U N A O U F L P S U A T Z I M
P O N O B Z T S T R T T E P P
M L T G V F I Y U O Z H X E E
F O Y A B M D U N R L B Z R C
T C Q U P A S S L W X P F C B
G W W C W C O U R A G E A Y W
B O H G E T O N U R B N C L B
```

◊ AKAMARU	◊ CHASE	◊ PAL
◊ ASTRO	◊ COLONEL	◊ PATOU
◊ AUGIE	◊ COURAGE	◊ PERCY
◊ BOLT	◊ DEPUTY DAWG	◊ PLUTO
◊ BRIAN	◊ GOOFY	◊ SPIKE
◊ BRUNO	◊ JOCK	◊ TYKE
◊ BUSTER	◊ LUIZ	◊ UNDERDOG
◊ BUTTONS	◊ MS. LION	◊ ZERO

```
D A R T A O C N I A R N R S J
T U B A L L L A U N C H E R L
T B C G T C V O R C S G A T E
E E S O R E O P J S D G L A P
N D E A L P K R O P E W K P O
N C T T M L U N E O O A U W R
I E L A H K A P A B P A T L D
S T H I E I R R P L G B S C E
B S K N C O N L H Y B E A D T
A A N W O K T G E A P R D G T
L E F D A U E N R I R A U R O
L B T W G E G R W I U N D K N
S E I T O O B R E C N P E S K
P K O V J K A R Y W F G C S V
O Y S Q U E A K Y B O N E V S
```

◊ BALL
  LAUNCHER

◊ BED

◊ BLANKET

◊ BOOTIES

◊ BOWL

◊ CAR SEAT

◊ CARRIER

◊ CLICKER

◊ COLLAR

◊ CRATE

◊ EAR WIPES

◊ GATE

◊ HARNESS

◊ KENNEL

◊ KNOTTED ROPE

◊ PET DOOR

◊ POOP BAG

◊ PUPPY PADS

◊ RAINCOAT

◊ SHAMPOO

◊ SQUEAKY
  BONE

◊ TEETHING RING

◊ TENNIS BALL

◊ TUG TOY

Excerpt from *Lad: A Dog* by Albert Terhune

Lady was as much a part of Lad's everyday happiness as the sunshine itself… Lad was an eighty-pound collie, thoroughbred in spirit as well as in blood. He had the benign dignity that was a heritage from endless generations of high-strain ancestors… His shaggy coat, set off by the snowy ruff and chest, was like orange-flecked mahogany. His absurdly tiny forepaws—in which he took inordinate pride— were silver white. Three years earlier, when Lad was in his first prime (before the mighty chest and shoulders had filled out and the tawny coat had waxed so shaggy), Lady had been brought to The Place. She had been brought in the Master's overcoat pocket, rolled up into a fuzzy gold-gray ball of softness no bigger than a half-grown kitten. The Master had fished the month-old puppy out of the cavern of his pocket and set her down, asprawl and shivering and squealing, on the veranda floor. Lad had walked cautiously across the veranda, sniffed inquiry at the blinking pigmy who gallantly essayed to growl defiance up at the huge welcomer—and from that first moment he had taken her under his protection.

```
E N S O R Y N A G O H A M D B
G O A U M E Y N W A T I N Y R
A I D T N K D E A N R P R W O
T T I R R S L N E T I I E O U
I C G E E L H M U G U A W N G
R E N V V P O I M Q S A U S H
E T I L A M R Y N H X C H R T
H O T I C Y S I I E G R O U E
K R Y S Z P D V D L W O R G C
I P H Z I E E T D E L S D E A
T N U R Y R S Y O F H S M G L
T F I A I E D C O L L I E U P
E T S N H A A N L Y R U S H R
N S G C L Y L R B P O C K E T
E Y P P U P S H S H A G G Y T
```

```
C W D C D D F T O B T C P T I
E Y Y U H R R B A L D A R E V
V S R R J D O M G A N Y E N P
A W O R R S B F R Z B E P R H
D G H R E E D L F E F N P A O
I S A O R H B Y E I E N O G E
R D K B N S C S R Z L E C W N
E G I N G E R E C M A C T J I
M R R S P J B A G O F H F O X
E H P L P A U T S O R I M D Y
Y R A N L T A N J T N A O J B
J U P L U C U O O E I I L S U
T S P M C V R B R A B U H R R
D T N A S W N K A S Y G R Y Y
V Y Y P O P P Y N O S M I R C
```

◊ AMBER	◊ CORAL	◊ PAPRIKA
◊ AUTUMN	◊ CRIMSON	◊ PHOENIX
◊ BERRY	◊ FIREBALL	◊ POPPY
◊ BLAZE	◊ FOX	◊ RHUBARB
◊ CAYENNE	◊ GARNET	◊ ROJO
◊ CHERRY	◊ GINGER	◊ ROSE
◊ CLIFFORD	◊ HAZEL	◊ RUBY
◊ COPPER	◊ MERIDA	◊ RUSTY

```
C O N T R A R Y B E L O V E D
R E H T A E W R E S U L T E D
E B D E C N A R F T O C S A M
T C E R E S N R E T T A P H C
Y L A I R T S U D N I A G L O
S F L P S M A L L N R U O S M
H Y O N S W R H T T O W T G P
A D N O E A C E M N N R U O A
D R G L G N L E E L O H L D C
E U L U E L N U I S S A A L T
S T E R E T W K H O R P I L R
L S F C O Y E O L G A P C U A
N A T U R E R O E A E Y O B M
V A R I E T Y T A C C E S S S
B S E C A F E T I P S E D B C
```

Group: Non-sporting/Utility

Background: Toy bulldogs were a mascot of sorts for Nottingham lace workers during the Industrial Revolution. Many took their beloved dogs with them when they left for France where crossbreeding resulted in the popular French bulldog.

Description: Slightly goofy in appearance, this small bulldog is recognizable by its large erect "bat ears". They are sturdy and compact with short coats in a variety of shades and patterns.

Temperament: Smart, courageous, and adaptable, their looks carry over into a clown-like, playful temperament. Their intellect and social nature mean they can do well in dog-agility despite appearances to the contrary, though their short-snouted faces mean they can easily over-exert themselves, especially in hot weather.

Energy Level: A short walk each day is enough for this small breed that is happy even in a flat or apartment home so long as there is access to a small outdoor space.

Dogs for Active and Outdoorsy People

```
C F G E N R E V E I R T E R N
T S D L A N B A E P T E M I A
W F W G M L T K O T T I J H I
E H B A R O H R O U X I W K T
I G Y E E C T L M E P R W A A
M L O B G U P A D I A I D R M
A L A D G O L B N K B D R E L
R E E U P A R S O R R G E L A
A S E S M E C O L L I E H I D
N S N L E H E T M V T B P A R
E U A D E N L H B I T A E N H
R R C R L G R C S Z A C H U J
P O I N T E R E I S N K S C Y
R J I D Y M W C B L Y K B U I
N A I L A R T S U A Y N J E W
```

◊ ALASKAN MALAMUTE

◊ AUSTRALIAN CATTLE DOG

◊ AUSTRALIAN SHEPHERD

◊ BEAGLE

◊ BERNESE MOUNTAIN DOG

◊ BORDER COLLIE

◊ BRITTANY

◊ DALMATIAN

◊ DOBERMAN PINSCHER

◊ GERMAN SHEPHERD

◊ GERMAN SHORTHAIRED POINTER

◊ JACK RUSSELL

◊ KARELIAN BEAR DOG

◊ LABRADOR RETRIEVER

◊ MIXED BREED

◊ PLOTT HOUND

◊ PORTUGUESE WATER DOG

◊ RHODESIAN RIDGEBACK

◊ SHETLAND SHEEPDOG

◊ SIBERIAN HUSKY

◊ VIZSLA

◊ WEIMARANER

```
K W A N E S E G N I K E P Y A
P G E R M A N B O E V N M E U
G U P I M E T O H N H A A K S
V L I A H S L S C O C I L R T
S Y P C R E A T I R I N T E R
N H W H C A I O B F W A E P A
O O I I O P E N I O R R S P L
L S O H F S S L V L O E E I I
L G P U T I P J U K N M N H A
I J E A B Z Y A I T C O A C N
P W K H F O U C A H H P V S H
A V O U A L R K V S P E A H T
P O F A S Y N D I D A F H P S
E L D O O P V S E P C H Y D T
Y O R E R I H S K R O Y L F H
```

◊ AUSTRALIAN TERRIER

◊ BICHON FRISE

◊ BORDER TERRIER

◊ BOSTON TERRIER

◊ CAIRN TERRIER

◊ CHIHUAHUA

◊ COTON DE TULEAR

◊ FRENCH BULLDOG

◊ GERMAN SPITZ

◊ HAVANESE

◊ JACK RUSSELL

◊ LHASA APSO

◊ LOWCHEN

◊ MALTESE

◊ NORFOLK TERRIER

◊ NORWICH TERRIER

◊ PAPILLON

◊ PEKINGESE

◊ POMERANIAN

◊ PUG

◊ SCHIPPERKE

◊ SHIH TZU

◊ TOY POODLE

◊ YORKSHIRE TERRIER

```
F C T E N A W K E G E V H V A
F N T J Y A T S D M R H O H I
O M B L K I I Y O H E E E M J
T U H A A A B C G A V U R E P
I I D W R Q O N W C O R D Y L
C N E P V U U T H R L N W O D
S S W K K I I P I Y L R E I I
S A H A A E T G S E O S M R S
E K E A V T R F T G R Y H L O
S P B A K R E T L D C P C B P
S B E T M E A I E N E R T L R
A L M I L U T P F V E B A K V
L N I S N L S O N M C C W T H
C K H R G A V R V G E B O A E
A C R G S P C D C L I C K E R
```

◊ BED	◊ HEEL	◊ SHAKE
◊ CLASSES	◊ LAP	◊ SIT
◊ CLICKER	◊ LEAVE IT	◊ SPEAK
◊ COME	◊ OFF	◊ STAY
◊ CRATE	◊ PLACE	◊ TAKE IT
◊ DOG WHISTLE	◊ PRAISE	◊ TREATS
◊ DOWN	◊ QUIET	◊ WAIT
◊ DROP IT	◊ ROLL OVER	◊ WATCH ME

```
I L W M S H T A B E E O S Y G
P W R B V A S K E M H H H N S
E O L K E B O E P S T T I P C
W A N B C M B O U A L N U L W
T I Y T N T O R E A I K E A C
S C N K A P B O E A C A W E S
N K S J R J P H R E N V O L U
S E Y N U W L T H G A U Y F N
M X H P S R A C R C S T D E S
T E E F N T Y H C K O O L D C
B R O T I E Z I L A I C O S R
I C F C S D N A M M O C I J E
B I K L E A W S N S S W B B E
D S O H T M I C R O C H I P N
L E E E L O T P C N D D N D I
```

◊ BRUSH TEETH

◊ CHECK FEET

◊ CLEAN EARS

◊ DE-FLEA

◊ EXERCISE

◊ GROOM

◊ HEALTHY DIET

◊ INSURANCE

◊ LOOK FOR TICKS

◊ MICROCHIP

◊ OCCASIONAL BATHS

◊ PICK UP POOP

◊ PLAY

◊ SOCIALIZE

◊ TAKE FOR WALKS

◊ TEACH COMMANDS

◊ TRAINING CLASSES

◊ TREAT INJURY

◊ USE SUNSCREEN

◊ VACCINATE

◊ VET CHECK-UPS

◊ WORM

Excerpt from *The Story of Doctor Dolittle* by Hugh Lofting

"Oh, don't talk so much," said Gub-Gub. "It's easy to talk; but it isn't so easy to find a man… You couldn't find the boy's uncle any more than the eagles could—you couldn't do as well."

"Couldn't I?" said the dog…

Then Jip went to the Doctor and said,

"Ask the boy if he has anything in his pockets that belonged to his uncle, will you, please?"

So the Doctor asked him…

Then the boy took from his pocket a great, big red handkerchief and said, "This was my uncle's too."

As soon as the boy pulled it out, Jip shouted,

"*Snuff*, by Jingo!—Black Rappee snuff. Don't you smell it? His uncle took snuff—Ask him, Doctor."

The Doctor questioned the boy again; and he said, "Yes. My uncle took a lot of snuff."

"Fine!" said Jip. "The man's as good as found. 'Twill be as easy as stealing milk from a kitten. Tell the boy I'll find his uncle for him in less than a week. Let us go upstairs and see which way the wind is blowing."

```
D S S E L O D O C T O R D F S
D E N O I T S E U Q W E E K N
R W S E E P P A R E G I D M U
F E I H C R E K D N A H L G F
Y L E A S Y D S O O N G N L F
E L G J D E R L D M N I L V W
N D I N T I E E I I L O T E A
I P U U A B L L H A J O U S S
F O O T A L K T E I O B N A K
F H S C U P Y T N K L U C E E
S P G P K N S G I O M L L L D
U D R B A E O T W N A M E P F
F N E W E F T I B L A C K M M
T I A A S E N S B U G B U G S
A W T Y N G Y O B N I A G A A
```

```
T C H S I F F O D N A T S J D
N R N E T A N O I T C E F F A
B R E E D S T S E D L O A O W
S M A L L I G U S Y L M C R R
N V S O A N S R G P I Q G E I
O F H U I T N T E L A N S H N
I M O T E E H A Y Q I C P E K
T E A D L L G Y I T U E E A L
A D R O I L U J N T R I A D E
L I A O G I O U G H P V R G D
U U H R A G H W A E E Y O E M
M M P G R E T P S R O D G W S
I L Y A M N S S Y C U R L E D
T C E R E T S R E G N A R T S
S L I A T E N E R G E T I C W
```

Group: Hound

Background: Dating back as far as the Egyptian pharaohs, this dog is perhaps one of the oldest living breeds.

Description: A small and lightly built hunting dog, the breed is very agile. They have erect ears, a wrinkled forehead, and curled tails.

Temperament: They are alert and intelligent dogs, and though independent they are affectionate to their family. They may be standoffish with strangers.

Energy Level: Though small this is an energetic breed that requires stimulation. They require a small to medium outdoor space.

```
G M A S R E T S A M Y S S F K
E P V C G N A I T E N E V P T
S T O O T N H K F O A M U R R
L B I F I A I B W Z M P I A R
E N E H R C E Y S H P A S R E
E B O A W I E O L Y L T H E T
P S A I T Z E Q N K Z U E A F
I E C L N R I N I F L O N R A
N S D F L U I Y D L E D V E K
G R G I L O E C Z N A D J A I
K E V E R R O G E N U G O N T
J T O Y G P E N C K N O W A C
Y N R I B R E I R R E T H I H
F U P A R E N T H O O D W V E
J H Z I N G K S O L R A C X N
```

- ◊ *A FRIEND IN NEED*
- ◊ *A GREY SPOTTED HOUND*
- ◊ *AFTER THE HUNT*
- ◊ *AREAREA*
- ◊ *BALLOON DOG*
- ◊ *DANCING DOGS*
- ◊ *DOG LYING IN SNOW*
- ◊ *HAPPY UNION*
- ◊ *LITTLE TERRIER*
- ◊ *MISS BEATRICE TOWNSEND*
- ◊ *NOEL IN THE KITCHEN*
- ◊ *PRIDE OF PARENTHOOD*
- ◊ *PRINCE CARLOS OF VIANA*
- ◊ *PUPPY*
- ◊ *SLEEPING DOG*
- ◊ *THE ARNOLFINI WEDDING*
- ◊ *THE DEATH OF ACTAEON*
- ◊ *THE HUNTERS IN THE SNOW*
- ◊ *THEIR MASTER'S VOICE*
- ◊ *TRIAL BY JURY*
- ◊ *TWO VENETIAN LADIES*
- ◊ *WHITE DOG*

```
Y L S E V I S O L P X E L N J
P R G R P N B Y H B M A R S F
A P A N C J R E Y I C E E N K
R M C R I A A R L I G A R A B
E E H R T D T L D F R E W E H
H O T I O N R E E C F A R F E
T W L A E I M E H H T U G J A
G I E S W S C E H C Z O R R R
M B J I I I U S H I A J K T I
G A M T L C R D E G U I D E N
H J U O S A O S T U O C S D G
A A P E B G R E V A D A C R E
F I R E A R M S O B H R C A J
G G F I T R A C K I N G U U D
D E L S Y T I L I B O M E G T
```

◊ AUTISM DOG

◊ BOMB DOG

◊ CADAVER DOG

◊ DRUG DOG

◊ EXPLOSIVES DOG

◊ FIREARMS DOG

◊ GUARD DOG

◊ GUIDE DOG

◊ HEARING DOG

◊ HERDING DOG

◊ MEDICAL RESPONSE DOG

◊ MILITARY DOG

◊ MOBILITY ASSISTANCE DOG

◊ POLICE DOG

◊ SCOUT DOG

◊ SEARCH AND RESCUE DOG

◊ SEIZURE ALERT DOG

◊ SENTRY DOG

◊ SLED DOG

◊ THERAPY DOG

◊ TRACKING DOG

◊ TRUFFLE DOG

◊ WATCHDOG

◊ WATER RESCUE DOG

```
T U N T S E H C K G Y D M I N
B I U B L D L K T B C E E B I
Y C O M Y N A G O H A M L R F
S E H P B E Y O A T I S P A F
H B N E L E C K B N T E A N U
T A O O W S R A J Y N C M D M
T R Z U H B L H E N U O O Y L
E H U E R L A T Y P Y C G C M
G F R F L B A C W T E D D Y O
Y U C R F L O M C A S B J R C
S D W O O L U N O A L Y E T H
F G O C P V E W E O F N M A A
A E O O T P E S W I S G U E R
M H S D W C E C O F F E E T J
C M S V N H N R K S I E N N A
```

◊ BEAR	◊ EWOK	◊ MUFFIN
◊ BOURBON	◊ FUDGE	◊ PENNY
◊ BRANDY	◊ HAZEL	◊ SCOOBY
◊ CHESTNUT	◊ HONEY	◊ SIENNA
◊ CHEWBACCA	◊ MAHOGANY	◊ TEDDY
◊ CHOCOLATE	◊ MAPLE	◊ TRUFFLES
◊ COCO	◊ MEATBALL	◊ UMBER
◊ COFFEE	◊ MOCHA	◊ WALNUT
◊ COPPER	◊ MOOSE	◊ WOODY

```
R K C O J Y K R A P S K Y R V
E G S P R P O J A K A U E Y J
G M D A N T E T L L N L C H Y
D M Y L O G I F L F L L I G P
O S L S M D E E N E E F A K T
D N E A R L T T Y F A I F D B
D D U E F S S D T J H S H Y Y
Y H P R F A L T N E F W G C J
P T M R B O Y I T L G H U R Y
F R A N C I S E N T S R M E F
N A P O L E O N T K I C O P O
W E N D B S U S L T Y T A E O
L U C K Y K P T A K E V O M G
L I T T L E B R O T H E R A P
P A E B G O M O Y T S U R X B
```

◊ BRUNO

◊ CHIEF

◊ DANTE

◊ DESOTO

◊ DODGER

◊ FRANCIS

◊ GEORGETTE

◊ GOOFY

◊ JOCK

◊ LADY

◊ LAFAYETTE

◊ LITTLE BROTHER

◊ LUCKY

◊ MAX

◊ NAPOLEON

◊ OLD YELLER

◊ PEG

◊ PERCY

◊ PERDITA

◊ RUSTY

◊ SCAMP

◊ SLINKY

◊ SPARKY

◊ STELLA

◊ TITO

Popular Breed Profile: Poodle (Standard)

```
I Y U S E D S T O C I R P A E
P M T B E S O G R O O M I N G
I N T E L L I G E N T A V M J
G C R T I E S A V R C E M O H
N B E F S R X K E T K C U D C
I R L R K A A E I A T K Y S A
D B D Y C L E V R S M N H R T
U S O L A G E L T C A O K E H
L E O R L A A A E M I S U T L
C R P U B R N N R G S S Y N E
N I A C I D K E W E R I E U T
I U N A A E G J C H L A H H I
O Q H R C N L C H N I Y L T C
H E D L S M A L L D E T T A M
I R E G U L A R E M O C E B A
```

Group: Non-sporting/Utility

Background: The poodle originated in Germany where it was used by duck hunters as a retriever.

Description: A medium-sized dog with a variety of coats including apricot, white, and black. Their curly hair can become matted and requires regular grooming.

Temperament: The standard poodle is a good-tempered, active, and intelligent breed.

Energy Level: The standard poodle is an athletic breed that requires a good amount of exercise, a large home, and access to at least a small garden.

43 Excerpt from *The Narrative of Arthur Gordon Pym* by Edgar Allan Poe

At my feet lay <u>crouched</u> a fierce <u>lion</u> of the <u>tropics</u>. Suddenly his wild eyes opened and <u>fell</u> upon me. With a <u>convulsive</u> bound he <u>sprang</u> to his <u>feet</u>, and laid bare his <u>horrible</u> teeth. In another instant there <u>burst</u> from his red <u>throat</u> a roar like the thunder of the firmament, and I fell impetuously to the <u>earth</u>. Stifling in a <u>paroxysm</u> of terror, I at last found <u>myself</u> partially <u>awake</u>. My <u>dream</u>, then, was not all a dream. Now, at least, I was in possession of my <u>senses</u>. The <u>paws</u> of some <u>huge</u> and real <u>monster</u> were pressing heavily upon my bosom—his hot <u>breath</u> was in my ear—and his white and <u>ghastly</u> <u>fangs</u> were gleaming upon me through the <u>gloom</u>… The <u>beast</u>, whatever it was, retained his <u>position</u> without attempting any immediate <u>violence</u>, while I lay in an utterly <u>helpless</u>, and, I <u>fancied</u>, a dying condition beneath him… but what was my astonishment, when, with a long and low <u>whine</u>, he commenced <u>licking</u> my <u>face</u> and <u>hands</u> with the <u>greatest</u> eagerness, and with the most extravagant demonstrations of <u>affection</u> and <u>joy</u>! I was bewildered, utterly <u>lost</u> in amazement— but I could not <u>forget</u> the peculiar whine of my Newfoundland dog <u>Tiger</u>, and the odd <u>manner</u> of his <u>caresses</u> I well knew. It was he.

T	S	R	U	B	B	S	S	E	L	P	L	E	H	H
C	H	U	G	E	M	O	R	E	T	S	N	O	M	T
A	G	H	A	S	T	L	Y	F	L	E	S	Y	M	A
R	C	S	E	L	B	I	R	R	O	H	G	O	I	E
E	T	N	O	I	T	C	E	F	F	A	O	R	V	R
S	S	S	C	O	T	E	E	F	R	L	T	I	O	B
S	T	F	R	N	S	D	B	K	G	E	S	G	N	F
E	V	I	O	L	E	N	C	E	A	L	G	N	O	S
S	H	S	U	I	S	M	M	E	U	W	N	I	I	C
W	T	D	C	O	N	A	A	V	R	H	A	K	T	I
A	R	N	H	L	E	Y	N	N	A	I	F	C	I	P
P	A	A	E	R	S	O	O	S	N	N	Y	I	S	O
F	E	H	D	E	C	A	F	J	F	E	L	L	O	R
T	H	R	O	A	T	M	S	Y	X	O	R	A	P	T
G	N	A	R	P	S	A	T	S	E	T	A	E	R	G

```
T Z H C K C A T S T R O H S T
R I S E S A M E J P O K I E U
I P A Y B H Y M R N S R T E P
U P J I L T F N E O E E U W I
Q Y T P E L G W I C B D N E L
S S I N E J O U J T U I H E L
Y T R M F F C D E C D P V P I
N F N A E B Y L L E J S M K L
I V B A M Y G M K E M I O Y E
S W R D B I H D L I R L K P Y
I L A M W B P B L H A N K D N
A A Y T G C M I S P E A N U T
R T L E J I Y M X H I C C U P
P O N I H C N G N I L P M U D
Y M P T S A C L W C E P C T A
```

◊ ATOM

◊ BITSY

◊ DOLLY

◊ DUMPLING

◊ ELF

◊ HICCUP

◊ JELLYBEAN

◊ LILLIPUT

◊ LOKI

◊ NYMPH

◊ PEANUT

◊ PEEWEE

◊ PIXIE

◊ RAISIN

◊ ROSEBUD

◊ SESAME

◊ SHORTSTACK

◊ SHRIMP

◊ SPIDER

◊ SQUIRT

◊ THIMBLE

◊ TINY

◊ TWIGLET

◊ ZIPPY

```
E S E N R E B W I Y U E S A R
V I J E R E T R I E V E R C E
M K G W O E I E B O S T O N X
U B P F L S L M R V U L C A O
F U R O H A F D L R L D H A B
G F M U A A B B O I I K J V G
O R D N S L V R E O E E O E S
D E O D L S S A A A P E R W R
L N C L N C E Z N D E X I M T
L C H A P W A L I E O O E R E
U H R N I F M E S V S R K H S
B V V D E R D R E H P E H S S
W K F O H E N C O C K E R C A
R E I L A V A C B E A G L E B
M E S I R F N O H C I B M Y P
```

- BASSET HOUND
- BEAGLE
- BERNESE MOUNTAIN DOG
- BICHON FRISE
- BORDER COLLIE
- BOSTON TERRIER
- BOXER
- BRUSSELS GRIFFON
- BULL TERRIER
- BULLDOG
- CAIRN TERRIER
- CAVALIER KING CHARLES
- COCKER SPANIEL
- FRENCH BULLDOG
- GERMAN SHEPHERD
- GOLDEN RETRIEVER
- HAVANESE
- IRISH SETTER
- LABRADOR
- MIXED BREED
- NEWFOUND-LAND
- POODLE
- PUG
- VIZSLA

Dogs That Need Big Homes – Part Two

```
Z O D N U O H R E T T O H E D
S D Q U A O K N W O Y G S U A
A N M S A M O Y E D E O U Q L
V U N R N J D L P V E R R A S
U O A E N A K O M O N D O R Z
K H H T A A I R B D U O H B I
P D G N Z Y I T H E C N G S V
C O F I I K N S A D R E A R W
N O A O B E I O E M S M E H S
S L J P I L G J F D L X A M P
A B I H G U O L S F O A P N I
L E M N B B H C R B I H D D N
U W E I M A R A N E R R R G O
K C H O W C H O W O W B G H N
I A I R E D E L A D E R I A E
```

◊ AFGHAN HOUND

◊ AIREDALE TERRIER

◊ BLOODHOUND

◊ BOXER

◊ BRAQUE D'AUVERGNE

◊ CHOW CHOW

◊ DALMATIAN

◊ DOBERMANN

◊ ENGLISH SETTER

◊ GORDON SETTER

◊ IBIZAN HOUND

◊ ITALIAN SPINONE

◊ KOMONDOR

◊ KORTHALS GRIFFON

◊ KUVASZ

◊ OTTERHOUND

◊ PHARAOH DOG

◊ POINTER

◊ RHODESIAN RIDGEBACK

◊ SALUKI

◊ SAMOYED

◊ SLOUGHI

◊ VIZSLA

◊ WEIMARANER

Popular Breed Profile: Beagle

```
E S I C R E X E A N C I E N T
E E S U O H S A Y D R U T S K
C L N T T A O C V A R I E T Y
H G D T R S K L A W D E E R B
I A I E N O Y R U T N E C A W
L E P S W E N W U H M Y S N Y
D B O P T O G G W S A E U G Q
R M N R Y S L I E A Y H O E Y
E O A A S M A L L E S T I R L
N C O H T S W Y A L R I R S D
E D E D N U O R R P E W U V N
D O O G T U R J G U V T C K E
Y R R E M U D E E H O U N D I
B A C K G R O U N D P H P I R
Y L I S A E N E R G E T I C F
```

Group: Hound

Background: The smallest British hound, as an ancient breed its background is somewhat difficult to trace but it was well established in England by the 15th century.

Description: A small but sturdy hound breed with a variety of coat variants, the beagle has long rounded ears, and reasonably large eyes.

Temperament: The word most associated with this breed is merry. They are friendly, curious, alert, and intelligent. Though occasionally standoffish with strangers, they are easily won over and are good with children.

Energy Level: Energetic and requiring an hour of exercise per day, the beagle is a breed that is happy in a small house with some outdoor space. A strong prey drive due to its hound nature means it should not be allowed off the leash on walks.

```
E P I T A P H G N I T I A W O
C Z H S S E N I P P A H I T G
D E T A I D E M N U R V Y N B
G G A L N A M D L O K O G E A
O B O R O T C I V Y C H A M G
D B Y D G T O P F S A U O E R
T R P R W V S M I L B N I V E
S A O H H E I C F K G S Y A D
O L W S A C N L C R T G R E R
L U E U M A A O E S T O R R O
T P R L R B L L S N U O A E B
R O R F A B T H E N H F U B H
A P G L H B A D D O G S Q O G
E G D W D O R A C L E A M E P
H L E C N E I R E P X E H L A
```

◊ *A DOG IN SAN FRANCISCO*

◊ *A POPULAR PARSONAGE AT HOME*

◊ *BAD DOGS*

◊ *BEAU*

◊ *BEREAVEMENT*

◊ *DHARMA*

◊ *DOG AROUND THE BLOCK*

◊ *EPITAPH TO A DOG*

◊ *GEIST'S GRAVE*

◊ *HALF BORDER AND HALF LAB*

◊ *LOST DOG*

◊ *MONGREL HEART*

◊ *OLD MAN, PHANTOM DOG*

◊ *ORACLE OF THE DOG*

◊ *THE DOG STOLTZ*

◊ *THE NEW DOG*

◊ *THE POWER OF THE DOG*

◊ *THE VICTOR DOG*

◊ *TO FLUSH, MY DOG*

◊ *TO THE QUARRY AND BACK*

◊ *UNMEDIATED EXPERIENCE*

◊ *WAITING FOR HAPPINESS*

```
S I O N I L A M B N Y E B O E
H T O O M S N A E G R O U G H
M P C R J U S R A N O O I C G
G A U C H O U I R M S H T C B
F L S C A V U C D T C U J O D
P L C E R F N S E U D N R H I
S E O E V C K I D V M D A H A
H I T L V U V O I I E F U B Y
E R C O V C E N G R F N J H A
B O H A R O J E J N T W G W B
R U S O G N I K B A L L E A I
I Z P J E L J E W A G O R C R
A C F A O F C A H N E I M P I
R M S O O F Y L K A H L A O H
D E K R E P P I H C S E N N C
```

◊ BEARDED COLLIE

◊ BORDER COLLIE

◊ BRIARD

◊ CAN DE CHIRA

◊ CAN DE PALLEIRO

◊ CANAAN DOG

◊ CHIRIBAYA DOG

◊ DUTCH SHEPHERD

◊ GAUCHO SHEEPDOG

◊ GERMAN SHEPHERD

◊ HUNTAWAY

◊ KOOLIE

◊ KUVASZ

◊ LAEKENOIS

◊ MALINOIS

◊ MCNAB

◊ MUDI

◊ ROUGH COLLIE

◊ SCHIPPERKE

◊ SCOTCH COLLIE

◊ SLOVAK CUVAC

◊ SMOOTH COLLIE

◊ TERVUREN

◊ TORNJAK

50 Excerpt from *Epitaph to a Dog* by Lord Byron

When some <u>proud</u> Son of Man <u>returns</u> to Earth,

Unknown to <u>Glory</u> but upheld by <u>Birth</u>,

The <u>sculptor's</u> art <u>exhausts</u> the pomp of <u>woe</u>,

And <u>storied</u> urns <u>record</u> who rests <u>below</u>.

When all is <u>done</u>, upon the <u>Tomb</u> is <u>seen</u>

Not <u>what</u> he was, but what he <u>should</u> have
  <u>been</u>.

But the <u>poor</u> Dog, in <u>life</u> the <u>firmest</u> friend,

The <u>first</u> to <u>welcome</u>, foremost to <u>defend</u>,

Whose <u>honest</u> heart is still his <u>Master's</u> own,

Who <u>labours</u>, fights, lives, <u>breathes</u> for him
  <u>alone</u>,

<u>Unhonour'd</u> falls, <u>unnotic'd</u> all his <u>worth</u>,

<u>Deny'd</u> in <u>heaven</u> the <u>Soul</u> he held on <u>earth</u>.

<u>While</u> man, vain <u>insect</u>! hopes to be <u>forgiven</u>,

And <u>claims</u> himself a sole <u>exclusive</u> heaven.

```
H T R A E D L U O H S E N O D
S P B E X H A U S T S P U C E
R Y R M C D C I T O N N U F I
U R F O L W O L E B H B I E R
O O O C U N L L U O S R B L O
B L R L S D S B N N M E E I T
A G G E I H C O A E I A N H S
L C I W V S U L S V T T O W S
U L V U E R L T D A R H L M N
U A E E D A P S H E P E A H R
B I N S E C T W C H N S P O U
I M F W V B O O W N T Y O N T
R S O A T S R I F E V P D E E
T E H T K D S D R E F I L S R
H D N E F E D S G B W O R T H
```

```
M E E A B R E C T S B L R N C
R C O C K E R B E H U O S S O
B E O W Y K A T I E L N O I D
O L N P A G T G S P L A T O C
S P O A I E W T L H D I E N O
T A I O R C A V E E O L R I O
O P J A D A A B E R G A V L N
N I N B U H M R I D R T U A H
E L E A S H O I D G D I R M O
N L S S T C A U E Y R L E S U
O O A S U F F U N W N O N R N
N N B E M D G U H D N K C A D
I S P T J A H G N I E E R T W
P O O D L E A A B U H U N D L
S M S Y B D N U H S H C A D M
```

◊ AFGHAN HOUND

◊ BASENJI

◊ BASSET HOUND

◊ BEAGLE

◊ BELGIAN MALINOIS

◊ BLOODHOUND

◊ BOSTON TERRIER

◊ BRACCO ITALIANO

◊ BULL TERRIER

◊ CHIHUAHUA

◊ COCKER SPANIEL

◊ DACHSHUND

◊ FRENCH BULLDOG

◊ GERMAN SHEPHERD

◊ IRISH SETTER

◊ ITALIAN SPINONE

◊ NORWEGIAN BUHUND

◊ PAPILLON

◊ PEMBROKE WELSH CORGI

◊ PICARDY SHEEPDOG

◊ POODLE

◊ TERVUREN

◊ TREEING WALKER COONHOUND

◊ WEIMARANER

```
Y K R Y N O N S G R I F F O N
K K C A J F I P Y V W B P E N
D O H S E T H I Q U E E A R O
Y N S R F L C T U J D D P I T
Y Y U P C E U Z A M C L I H S
K F E H A R P T E E E I L S O
S K D G L A E D E S I N L K B
E E A Y U L S S H D E G O R E
C S C V X P A A T S N T N O Y
N E H C W O L V H E J O L Y U
K N S M E E F I V L D N T A R
P A H A A U H A U H I H C O M
W V U U S T O Y P O O D L E C
R A N T Z E S E G N I K E P M
D H D U H I J N E S A B D U I
```

◊ BASENJI

◊ BEDLINGTON TERRIER

◊ BOSTON TERRIER

◊ BRUSSELS GRIFFON

◊ CESKY TERRIER

◊ CHIHUAHUA

◊ CHINESE CRESTED

◊ COTON DE TULEAR

◊ FINNISH SPITZ

◊ FOX TERRIER

◊ HAVANESE

◊ JACK RUSSELL

◊ JAPANESE CHIN

◊ LHASA APSO

◊ LOWCHEN

◊ MALTESE

◊ MINIATURE DACHSHUND

◊ PAPILLON

◊ PEKINGESE

◊ PUG

◊ SHIH TZU

◊ SWEDISH VALLHUND

◊ TOY POODLE

◊ YORKSHIRE TERRIER

Popular Breed Profile: Pembroke Welsh Corgi

```
E K O R B M E P R I C K E D C
L C I A E M Y T E I R A V G O
A O Y G C I N V I T A T I O N
I R R I H E J B U I L D G J T
C G N L O L B R E E D I N G I
A I E I I U T S E Y E A O N N
F C H T C D E O T V T O R I U
E I B Y E E S H U U E S T D E
T T E T I H W N R T R L S R D
A E K M R C O E R S G D C E D
R L C H W S L U J E E O Y H L
E H A F L E M I S H T L I L O
D T L D E R I U Q E R T A N B
O A B S B E L O V E D M A W G
M Q U E E N E L B A S E L P Y
```

Group: Herding/Pastoral

Background: Flemish weavers came to Wales in 1107 at the invitation of Henry I, bringing their dogs. Through breeding these dogs became the Pembroke Welsh corgi. Its royal patronage has continued as they have been beloved pets of Queen Elizabeth II.

Description: Low-set but sturdy and strong in build, this little dog has pricked ears and round eyes giving it a fox-like facial appearance. They have a variety of coat patterns such as black and tan, fawn and white, red and white, and sable.

Temperament: Affectionate, bold, alert, and clever. Their outgoing and friendly nature combined with athleticism often makes them a great choice for canine agility.

Energy Level: Though small, this breed was built for herding and is athletic, requiring a moderate walking schedule, and will even happily accompany you on a slow jog. A house with some outdoor space is required.

```
B O J J L F K H A N N I B A L
H C T E F R F M K A N I N E T
M C N M E S K Y W A L K I E S
L D O N W A K R A B W E H C Y
L R T O N O K C O L R E H S Y
H O V T P W O O F H O U S E E
N Y O I E E N F V K M S A I L
E O M R G H H C S T B B V N S
S L F U D J R T A T O K H D A
N P G F O O W O E B E U O I E
I A G A U L H W B I Y R M A L
P W N U E U E V I O N E S N F
P T M K N B M U T T A N A A A
U E U T I H C T A R C S I H E
P R H C T H E M U T T R A W Y
```

◊ ALLY MCBEAGLE

◊ ATTICUS FETCH

◊ BARK RENTON

◊ BEOWOOF

◊ BERTIE WOOFSTER

◊ BILBO WAGGINS

◊ BOB SCRATCHIT

◊ BOBA FETCH

◊ CHEWBARKA

◊ CITIZEN KANINE

◊ EMMA WOOFHOUSE

◊ HAIRY PAWTER

◊ HANNIBAL LICKTER

◊ INDIANA BONES

◊ JABBA THE MUTT

◊ LUKE SKYWALKIES

◊ MARY PUPPINS

◊ NANCY DROOL

◊ RHETT MUTTLER

◊ RON FLEASLEY

◊ SHERLOCK BONES

◊ TONY MUTTANA

◊ WINNIE-THE-POOCH

```
T R A E B D A H L I A T T G E
X Y T S M O K E N B E M E U C
B A U K X O N Y X L A P F J I
H S A L H U L S L A T E R M R
C T P H A N T O M C P F E U O
I D A R T H L T I K J B B M U
G J C S Y O N H E W W W M W Q
A R M S N X E G C I N D E R I
M E I E M J A I W D Y R G V L
K D D N S H M L U O Y T O O S
C N N N M M R I A W D W S I E
A U I I U V O W E G W A O I V
L H G U D L T T L F M V H R M
B T H G G R S C O S M O S S C
M B T E E E O P E P P E R H S
```

◊ ASH	◊ GALAXY	◊ SHADOW
◊ BEAR	◊ GUINNESS	◊ SLATE
◊ BLACK MAGIC	◊ JET	◊ SMOKE
◊ BLACK WIDOW	◊ LIQUORICE	◊ SMUDGE
◊ CINDER	◊ MIDNIGHT	◊ SOOTY
◊ COSMOS	◊ MISTY	◊ STORM
◊ CROW	◊ ONYX	◊ STYX
◊ DAHLIA	◊ PEPPER	◊ THUNDER
◊ DARTH	◊ PHANTOM	◊ TUX
◊ EMBER	◊ POE	◊ TWILIGHT

```
W J J W D B E G C Y J J K E G
A D M U D U H T M E P V E E G
L F L O W O C R G P V H R L H
T N T T R M O K F F D A T B I
U F R S R T U C F B C U D U G
O F E A S A M L A O J N L O H
T E S J J O I M L Y O T I R P
G J C C C N H L G I O T W T A
J G U E O O H O I A G T E B S
D N E S U C D S D N W A R D S
E I E N J W O F I O G O N E C
S D D G O G M Y D R T I D R U
E A N N T F T O O H I L B G A
R R S D E M G V E T L O C I I
T T M V F S H R V S E C R B P
```

◇ BIG RED

◇ A NOSE FOR
  TROUBLE

◇ COYOTE SONG

◇ DAVE AND
  HIS DOG,
  MULLIGAN

◇ DESERT DOG

◇ HAUNT FOX

◇ IRISH RED

◇ LION HOUND

◇ OUTLAW RED

◇ RESCUE
  DOG OF THE
  HIGH PASS

◇ SNOW DOG

◇ STORMY

◇ THE
  DUCK-FOOTED
  HOUND

◇ TRADING JEFF
  AND HIS DOG

◇ TRAILING
  TROUBLE

◇ TWO DOGS
  AND A HORSE

◇ WILD TREK

◇ WOLF
  BROTHER

Excerpt from *Beautiful Joe* by Marshall Saunders

My name is <u>Beautiful</u> Joe, and I am a <u>brown</u>
dog of <u>medium</u> size. I am not called Beautiful
<u>Joe</u> because I am a <u>beauty</u>... When my <u>mistress</u>
went every year to <u>register</u> me and pay my <u>tax</u>,
and the man in the <u>office</u> asked what <u>breed</u>
I was, she said part <u>fox-terrier</u> and part bull-
terrier; but he always put me down a <u>cur</u>. I don't
think she <u>liked</u> having him call me a cur; still, I
have <u>heard</u> her say that she <u>preferred</u> curs, for
they have more <u>character</u> than well-bred <u>dogs</u>.
Her father said that she liked ugly dogs for the
same <u>reason</u> that a <u>nobleman</u> at the <u>court</u> of a
<u>certain</u> king did namely, that no one else would.

I am an <u>old</u> dog now, and am <u>writing</u>, or rather
getting a <u>friend</u> to write, the story of my life. I
have <u>seen</u> my mistress <u>laughing</u> and <u>crying</u> over
a little <u>book</u> that she says is a story of a <u>horse's</u>
life, and <u>sometimes</u> she puts the book <u>down</u>
close to my nose to let me see the <u>pictures</u>.

I <u>love</u> my dear mistress; I can say no <u>more</u> than
that; I love her <u>better</u> than any one <u>else</u> in the
<u>world</u>; and I think it will <u>please</u> her if I write the
<u>story</u> of a dog's <u>life</u>.

```
J S X K L M I S T R E S S K N
E A O I D R C M D R A E H W A
T O K M N Y E H N E E S O P E
B E J N E M O A A C V R L I F
D S Q A I T E F S R B O D C O
E A R M R L I D F O A H B T X
R E E E F A L M I I N C E U T
R L G L E U V U E U C Y T R E
E P I B Y G T W F S M E T E R
F F S O R H R R D I R Y E S R
E E T N O I U J U O T S R L I
R V E M T N K E M O W U G E E
P O R I S G N I Y R C N A O R
D L N C E R T A I N B R E E D
U G Y T U A E B O D L R O W B
```

Popular Breed Profile: German Shepherd

```
K E W T H E B I R C S E D S K
B O S O Y G A R D E N Y U U O
N E U H R R Y T E I R A V O E
B R F C O K U S T E A D Y E C
S N A I L U I T A L A T E G I
N I N E T O S N N L F G E A L
R A A I L T S E G E R W V R O
E L M A N Z I E D A C M I U P
T P R D W C Z N L E B I T O G
T C E R E K L U G Y T L C C N
A W G O W T P U M J B I A F O
P O L A Y O L S D R W T U C L
D R E H P E H S E E E A R S K
V D T S R I F E S I C R E X E
E S P H E R D I N G F Y J D N
```

Group: Herding/Pastoral

Background: First developed as a herding dog in the late 19th century, the German shepherd is now most closely associated with being a working breed in military and police roles.

Description: Usually black and tan or plain black in a variety of patterns, the German shepherd is a medium-large dog with large erect ears and a long muzzle.

Temperament: Befitting a popular military dog, the words frequently used to describe the German shepherd include loyal, steady, self-assured, and courageous.

Energy Level: An active dog requiring two hours of exercise a day, this breed is best suited to a large house and garden.

```
Y N W V S S E N K R A D W C F
G E S S E L D N E J G L F A H
L E O D T M R I V E R O L B R
U R L T A L P H A S K L R E N
C G A H T Y K T R B S U J I B
K B N I G H T T Y R N B O F O
Y F O W Y S H A D O W S U L S
E J O N L E A Y H K S D R A F
S N O R U N K A O E M E N B B
A S I O E R M C O N A D E A D
K H L H E S H R I H Y I Y D R
O P T T S O T W O M F V A T A
K N N R I N M O E T J I D V K
W U V C A H U N T U S D S I A
H L E U D M E S E Y F F F S B
```

◊ *A HIDDEN ENEMY*

◊ *A PACK DIVIDED*

◊ ALFIE

◊ *ALPHA'S TALE*

◊ BELLA

◊ BRUNO

◊ DAISY

◊ *DARKNESS FALLS*

◊ *DEAD OF NIGHT*

◊ ERIN HUNTER

◊ FOREST

◊ *INTO THE SHADOWS*

◊ JULIA GREEN

◊ LUCKY

◊ MARTHA

◊ MICKEY

◊ *MOON'S CHOICE*

◊ RIVER

◊ *STORM OF DOGS*

◊ SUNSHINE

◊ *SWEET'S JOURNEY*

◊ *THE BROKEN PATH*

◊ *THE EMPTY CITY*

◊ *THE ENDLESS LAKE*

◊ *THE FINAL BATTLE*

◊ THORN

```
C O I W G E O O P A K E E P W
A O S G J A C K A B E E G G E
V P L C R I O O P I K R O Y L
A E O A O O P A K C O C L C D
P I E M B N D U V F W N D H O
O T G L C R I J U J O L E O O
O S E V G H A L B H R R N R D
O E R L B G I D C S E T D K A
P W E I D I U U O H C P O I P
A B G C H O Z P C O G R O E E
M M O S L S O R V U D E D P E
O M L T E R U N J P E L L R H
P A L R E L E E H S A X E T S
M A L T I P O O U C C H U G Y
R E I L G A E B K O S I J N H
```

◊ BEAGLIER

◊ CAVAPOO

◊ CHORKIE

◊ CHUG

◊ COCKAPOO

◊ DORGI

◊ GOLDEN-
  DOODLE

◊ JACKABEE

◊ JUG

◊ LABRADOODLE

◊ LURCHER

◊ MAL-SHI

◊ MALTIPOO

◊ PEEKAPOO

◊ POMAPOO

◊ POMCHI

◊ PUGGLE

◊ SCHNOODLE

◊ SHEEPA-
  DOODLE

◊ TEXAS HEELER

◊ WESTIEPOO

◊ YORKIPOO

◊ ZUCHON

Name Ideas for Big Dogs – Part One

```
B R T E K U D A M R A M W J A
S H I S W U S A W S D O Y J C
S C A M A Z O N D C L W V G C
E O F K I E S E A V C E A K A
H O F G W A B E E X F I O C B
C H I E F B S R E T A R A G W
U M L N F A I R H I A J E T E
D L C A R N X K D N N N O B H
M Y H N E E C L G Y E G C P C
R M T A S S O A U R L L N H F
O M A O J U R W A C O R F A N
C U E J J T Y L W N I L J A F
K A H S O U F B D E W F A V F
Y O T G N R T O N J W O E A C
R O H T T B N N T T H D I R J
```

◊ AMAZON	◊ GAIA	◊ MARMADUKE
◊ BEAST	◊ GENERAL	◊ NANA
◊ BRUTUS	◊ HEATHCLIFF	◊ RAGNAROK
◊ CAESAR	◊ HOOCH	◊ ROCKY
◊ CHEWBACCA	◊ JET	◊ THOR
◊ CHIEF	◊ LONDON	◊ TINY
◊ DUCHESS	◊ LUCIFER	◊ WOLVERINE
◊ FANG	◊ MAJOR	◊ XERXES

```
A T B J C H E S A P E A K E U
H U G F L A T C O A T E D S W
Y C D N U O H R E T T O K C R
S P A N I E L O H S I R I H R
L N A M R E G N I L L O T I E
A D P O R T U G U E S E S P T
B R I T T A N Y N R N A T P R
R E K C O C W G B E L L A E I
A N L U C P L A D S B A N R E
D T A C J I R L Z O D B D K V
O S G U S B O I Y V T R A E E
O C O H E G V K T M S A R P R
D H T T P O I N T E R D D A I
L E T P O N O V A S C O T I A
E C O D E T A O C Y L R U C O
```

◊ BARBET

◊ BOYKIN SPANIEL

◊ BRITTANY

◊ CHESAPEAKE BAY RETRIEVER

◊ COCKER SPANIEL

◊ CURLY-COATED RETRIEVER

◊ DRENTSCHE PATRIJSHOND

◊ ENGLISH SETTER

◊ FLAT-COATED RETRIEVER

◊ GERMAN SHORTHAIRED POINTER

◊ GOLDEN RETRIEVER

◊ IRISH WATER SPANIEL

◊ LABRADOODLE

◊ LABRADOR

◊ LAGOTTO ROMAGNOLO

◊ NOVA SCOTIA DUCK TOLLING RETRIEVER

◊ OTTERHOUND

◊ PORTUGUESE WATER DOG

◊ SCHIPPERKE

◊ STANDARD POODLE

◊ VIZSLA

```
P G E K A R O S S E F O R P N
T K O T I A R I K A Y H V O E
J U P I T E R V D V D T M I Y
H O B R E H R T K B N U Y G K
E A N D E R S O N I R E X O C
F B N S S O B M M A V T N R H
S U A W W E M R U R V A C A I
N F S N G R E T A R Y F B O E
O F A O A P U H B R R A A R F
S E U N P T O G B A L A B A N
L J K E M R A N U J E L Y C S
E I P D U K E W P A R C S L J
N E H A I B G E M T U N N E G
R G O N D O N O N O T R O N V
O M G S P O T S T R A C Y H I
```

◊ AKIRA ITO

◊ BILL MURRAY

◊ BOB BALABAN

◊ BOSS

◊ BRYAN CRANSTON

◊ CHIEF

◊ DUKE

◊ EDWARD NORTON

◊ GONDO

◊ GRETA GERWIG

◊ HARVEY KEITEL

◊ IGOR

◊ INTERPRETER NELSON

◊ JEFF GOLDBLUM

◊ JUPITER

◊ KEN WATANABE

◊ KING

◊ KOYU RANKIN

◊ KUNICHI NOMURA

◊ NUTMEG

◊ ORACLE

◊ PEPPERMINT

◊ PROFESSOR WATANABE

◊ REX

◊ SCRAP

◊ SPOTS

◊ TRACY WALKER

◊ WES ANDERSON

64

Excerpt from *The Hound of the Baskervilles*
by Sir Arthur Conan Doyle

Twice I have with my own ears heard the sound which resembled the distant baying of a hound. It is incredible, impossible, that it should really be outside the ordinary laws of nature. A spectral hound which leaves material footmarks and fills the air with its howling is surely not to be thought of. Stapleton may fall in with such a superstition, and Mortimer also, but if I have one quality upon earth it is common sense, and nothing will persuade me to believe in such a thing. To do so would be to descend to the level of these poor peasants, who are not content with a mere fiend dog but must needs describe him with hell-fire shooting from his mouth and eyes. Holmes would not listen to such fancies, and I am his agent. But facts are facts, and I have twice heard this crying upon the moor. Suppose that there were really some huge hound loose upon it; that would go far to explain everything. But where could such a hound lie concealed, where did it get its food, where did it come from, how was it that no one saw it by day? It must be confessed that the natural explanation offers almost as many difficulties as the other.

```
N I A L P X E E R I F L L E H
C D C W A A D E S C E N D O K
D A N K G R T H L S E M L O H
E N L E A R T H J D U C R D N
L O N M I U D C A N R O N R G
A T O C O F F U E Y O N A A N
E E J M R S S A I P E F T E I
C L D B A R T N N S S E U H H
N P N I E T G N O C E S R T T
O A U P S N E P A C I S A N Y
C T O S I T P R I T R E L A R
S S H L T U U W I O U D S T E
U U W E S A T O O A I R D S V
C O M O R T I M E R L E E I E
H I S E I T L U C I F F I D E
```

```
G A L E O N B E R G F E M R E
C O N F I D E N T F E U E H B
O R D H L U F Y A L P C L Y E
A I E A G N I K I R T S L L L
T G S N B L A C K A B I S Y Y
Y I I G E R M A N Y M S G O I
L N C I N U Y G N A T U R E N
L A R N V E U L F E G O O L G
A L E G E L D W D E M R W B E
R L X V A K Y R N N B O N U N
E Y E R G E S T A I E G H O I
N M U S C U L A R G E I O D N
E M L A C E A C M D K V R L O
G W P E C N A R A E P P A F E
A S E R E N E U D E E R B V L
```

Group: Working

Background: Originally used as a guard dog and bred to have a "leonine" or "lion-like" appearance, this big dog originates from the town of Leonberg in Germany.

Description: A large, muscular breed that is calm and confident, it has a long, double coat, and a somewhat rectangular head with medium-sized hanging ears and a striking black mask.

Temperament: Belying its large appearance, this large dog is a gentle giant and is generally calm, friendly, and playful. Its serene nature makes it an excellent family pet.

Energy Level: Though generally calm when fully grown, this big breed requires vigorous exercise, with a large home and garden space.

```
N I K Y O B I R E W E I B U I
L I C V J R R B C H I N E S E
C O J A R S R D I T G B S D K
N A M N T P H E K Z U A W O K
A S R N E A R V G Y A I O G Z
I S T O A S H N L T U N L S Y
L T Y A L E A O G C I T A L K
E C H Y B I N B U H A V G A E
R I V P M Y N E C L U K O E D
A R C O V C H A R K A E T K E
K N L I N K I O O Y D I T E T
N E T K L D U H U S P P O N M
T C H S Y U I I R N T L V O U
P O S C H A P E N D O E S I D
Y E Y K S L O U G H I K U S I
```

◊ AUSTRALIAN KELPIE

◊ BASENJI

◊ BELGIAN LAEKENOIS

◊ BIEWER TERRIER

◊ BOYKIN SPANIEL

◊ CAROLINA DOG

◊ CATAHOULA LEOPARD DOG

◊ CHINESE CRESTED

◊ CHINOOK

◊ CIRNECO DELL'ETNA

◊ CZECHO-SLOVAKIAN VLCAK

◊ IBIZAN HOUND

◊ KARELIAN BEAR DOG

◊ KUVASZ

◊ LAGOTTO ROMAGNOLO

◊ MUDI

◊ OVCHARKA

◊ PULI

◊ PYRENEAN SHEPHERD

◊ SCHAPENDOES

◊ SKYE TERRIER

◊ SLOUGHI

◊ STABYHOUN

◊ TELOMIAN

```
D W I D R E I R R E T T A R W
U E H D A L M A T I A N O M E
H R X I D R E H P E H S W R I
Z P E I P Y K S U H I B G E M
S R A K M P S I U J D E N Z A
H O R R C O E T R A N Y O U R
E D P E A O Z T E C U E L A A
T A N N Q D C O D K O S L N N
L R E O Q L T C R R H E I H E
A B D B T E W S O U Y N P C R
N A L D E T O A B S E I A S E
D L O E M Q O K V S R H P U T
U J G R H N Q G E E G C S S Z
E I P L E K J M A L I N O I S
I T V I Z S L A P L M M N E H
```

◊ AUSTRALIAN KELPIE

◊ BELGIAN MALINOIS

◊ BORDER COLLIE

◊ CHINESE CRESTED

◊ COCKER SPANIEL

◊ DALMATIAN

◊ GERMAN SHEPHERD

◊ GOLDEN RETRIEVER

◊ GREYHOUND

◊ JACK RUSSELL

◊ LABRADOR

◊ LAGOTTO ROMAGNOLO

◊ MINIATURE SCHNAUZER

◊ MIXED BREED

◊ PAPILLON

◊ POODLE

◊ RAT TERRIER

◊ REDBONE COONHOUND

◊ SCOTTISH TERRIER

◊ SHETLAND SHEEPDOG

◊ SIBERIAN HUSKY

◊ VIZSLA

◊ WEIMARANER

◊ WHIPPET

```
L O D N A L D N U O H W E N L
I Y T W D O G O M I T E S G W
C H W W P S M O R Y S T A U O
K W A Y A A G I U S D I O U O
T D P E A P R U A A N S A H F
E G A L B R A H D A I B D S S
N V G E C E A M B V A T A I T
S K N K A L L L A R O P N D E
T P I R I T W A K N A B E A R
E U S A E O A C R W I B R G P
I P T B H Y E B T U R K R O E
N U N K C L A U A D F D R D G
M A I L O R G N O M E F G A D
T P N N K A Y A R A B K R A B
B F A U L H O U N D U R A S O
```

◊ BARK-CELONA

◊ BARKELEY

◊ BARKINA FASO

◊ BARKU

◊ BELARUFF

◊ DOGADISHU

◊ GRRRENADA

◊ HOUNDURAS

◊ HOWLBANIA

◊ LICKTENSTEIN

◊ MAPAWTO

◊ MONGROLIA

◊ NEWHOUND-
LAND

◊ PAWTUGAL

◊ PUPUA NEW
GUINEA

◊ SANTA
BARKBARA

◊ SINGAPAW

◊ TAILAHASSEE

◊ THE
DOGOMITES

◊ WOOFSTER

Don't Feed to Dogs

```
S E T A L O C O H C S E F C L
E K J L S R A I S I N S W O F
L G H M M G E C E A A W W O E
O C B O U R I H H T L B N K N
H O F N L A S P C I O O M E O
O F R D P N S A A C V A C D M
C F B S O S V E E C E E N B M
L E N I D O G H P R J U S O I
A E N W C A T J C A T M K N S
E O D A R N N E E M R M I E R
D T D L O S C I E P J G I S E
B O I N C I N G J D F E T L P
S C R B L O T I L Y X E D A K
D O M A C A D A M I A N U T S
C J V R E D W O P G N I K A B
```

◊ ALCOHOL

◊ ALMONDS

◊ AVOCADOS

◊ BAKING POWDER

◊ CHIVES

◊ CHOCOLATE

◊ COFFEE

◊ COOKED BONES

◊ CORN ON THE COB

◊ GARLIC

◊ GRAPES

◊ ICE CREAM

◊ MACADAMIA NUTS

◊ MILK

◊ NUTMEG

◊ ONIONS

◊ PEACHES

◊ PERSIMMON

◊ PLUMS

◊ RAISINS

◊ TEA

◊ XYLITOL

Popular Breed Profile: Border Collie

T	G	L	B	C	I	T	S	E	M	O	D	H	T	M
T	N	E	T	R	W	S	A	B	E	E	E	R	V	E
E	I	N	S	O	E	G	M	C	R	R	E	V	R	D
X	K	G	O	S	I	E	N	E	D	L	I	E	E	I
T	R	T	M	L	N	E	D	I	A	S	C	S	S	U
U	O	H	I	T	I	I	N	H	R	T	T	D	E	M
R	W	T	A	D	S	G	B	E	S	H	E	N	R	D
E	Y	L	E	N	R	E	G	N	O	L	X	E	V	V
S	B	B	O	P	T	N	R	U	L	U	C	R	E	I
I	O	C	U	T	A	E	G	I	S	H	E	D	D	G
C	R	P	E	R	T	H	F	O	V	A	L	L	K	O
R	D	R	T	T	Y	L	I	M	A	F	S	I	S	R
E	E	S	A	O	U	T	S	I	D	E	H	H	A	O
X	R	P	C	F	E	R	E	S	R	A	O	C	T	U
E	N	E	R	G	E	T	I	C	H	T	O	O	M	S

Group: Herding/Pastoral

Background: Still often seen herding sheep, the task for which they were originally bred, the border collie is considered one of the most intelligent domestic dog breeds.

Description: A medium breed with a variety of coat patterns in two textures, smooth—short and coarser and medium length—softer and longer but not excessively so. They have alert, oval eyes and medium-sized semi-erect/erect ears.

Temperament: A tenacious, energetic, alert, and intelligent breed, this whip-smart pup excels in most canine activities, from herding and obedience to tracking and agility. Affectionate with their family, they can be reserved with strangers and their desire to herd means they are better in a home with older children.

Energy Level: Though they are fine in a small house, this energetic working breed requires vigorous daily exercise and a large outside space, as well as mental engagement to live a fulfilled life.

Excerpt from *The Wizard of Oz* by L. Frank Baum

It was <u>Toto</u> that made <u>Dorothy</u> <u>laugh</u>, and <u>saved</u> her from growing as <u>gray</u> as her other surroundings. Toto was not gray; he was a <u>little</u> <u>black</u> dog, with long silky hair and small black eyes that <u>twinkled</u> merrily on either side of his <u>funny</u>, wee nose. Toto <u>played</u> all day long, and Dorothy played with him, and <u>loved</u> him <u>dearly</u>…

From the far <u>north</u> they heard a low <u>wail</u> of the wind, and Uncle <u>Henry</u> and Dorothy could <u>see</u> where the long <u>grass</u> bowed in <u>waves</u> before the coming <u>storm</u>…

Aunt Em <u>dropped</u> her <u>work</u> and came to the door. One <u>glance</u> told her of the danger <u>close</u> at hand. "<u>Quick</u>, Dorothy!" she <u>screamed</u>. "<u>Run</u> for the <u>cellar</u>!"

Toto <u>jumped</u> out of Dorothy's <u>arms</u> and <u>hid</u> <u>under</u> the bed, and the girl <u>started</u> to get him. Aunt Em, <u>badly</u> frightened, <u>threw</u> open the trap door in the floor and climbed down the <u>ladder</u> into the <u>small</u>, dark hole. Dorothy caught Toto at last and started to <u>follow</u> her aunt. When she was <u>halfway</u> across the room there came a great <u>shriek</u> from the wind, and the <u>house</u> <u>shook</u> so hard that she lost her <u>footing</u> and sat down <u>suddenly</u> upon the <u>floor</u>.

```
D E Y A L P R L Y W O L L O F
K D R O P P E D I A T G I R P
C Y L D A B S H C T W O R A N
I B W E R H T G J L T F T A W
U L A A R M S U L Y O L L O Y
Q A V I D E M A E R C S E A D
W C E R S P M L G N E R E E H
E K S U E S V N U E L G T S Y
C I O D S D I R F H L R Y U H
N H M S L T N D E V A S L D T
A A A O O N O U W T R H R D O
L R V O O W B R S O I O A E R
G E F R O O L F M D R O E N O
D S T D E L K N I W T K D L D
H H L A D D E R F U N N Y Y D
```

```
V W N B F P S E C I J L O H Z
T L B K R Y I E T I H L R K C
Y S I A D L O G H E L D U K Q
S F R R R L U R Y A E U B C F
T D K A D O E E F K J K Y G Y
E I H C E M Q V T F C E E B M
L C H S A B A I L E Y O U T O
L C K O A J Y L Y Q D D R X V
A F M C F L S O V D D D F Y S
S G P A U K E O V Y B Z Y E Q
Z E O L Z Q U I P C B E L L A
H I E F L A Q A D H H F Y R E
F S A I P E N N Y A I L M A C
W O R E P O O C X B S E O H Y
B R W B R Y P B W E J S Z E J
```

◊ ALFIE	◊ DAISY	◊ PENNY
◊ BAILEY	◊ DUKE	◊ ROCKY
◊ BEAR	◊ HARLEY	◊ ROSIE
◊ BELLA	◊ JACK	◊ RUBY
◊ BUDDY	◊ LUCY	◊ SADIE
◊ CHARLIE	◊ MOLLY	◊ SOPHIE
◊ CHLOE	◊ OLIVER	◊ STELLA
◊ COOPER	◊ OSCAR	◊ TEDDY

```
G B P A P I L L O N D K J M V
N P I W F E L U G R Y N P N K
A A O E C R K J E J I O E A J
P E U M W G R I F F O N F I A
B S W H E E R E N D O F I L P
I E F T A R R U L G E H L A A
C N F A E U A E S N E O R R N
H G R T R U H N P S W S L T E
O O Y C O H S I I C I M E S S
N L I J W I N D H A I A I U E
F O C R E S T E D C N L N A N
R B F N C T N V M S H T A R A
I K D H O R A E L U T E P W V
S E E N G L I S H U V S S B A
E R G U P D N U O H Y E R G H
```

◇ AFFEN-
PINSCHER

◇ AUSTRALIAN
SILKY TERRIER

◇ BICHON FRISE

◇ BIEWER
TERRIER

◇ BOLOGNESE

◇ BRUSSELS
GRIFFON

◇ CHIHUAHUA

◇ CHINESE
CRESTED

◇ COTON DE
TULEAR

◇ ENGLISH TOY
TERRIER

◇ HAVANESE

◇ ITALIAN
GREYHOUND

◇ JAPANESE CHIN

◇ KING CHARLES
SPANIEL

◇ LOWCHEN

◇ MALTESE

◇ PAPILLON

◇ PEKINGESE

◇ POMERANIAN

◇ PUG

◇ RUSSIAN TOY

◇ TOY POODLE

◇ YORKSHIRE
TERRIER

```
Y L H S I G G O D G O D K R D
D O G W K J D O G G O N E O K
O E N A V G O D G G W H G B G
G O I N H M O Y M D C S K E D
D K D O G G Y A D T S R L P O
O T D D O G T D A E M G T D G
G D E O O I O C N D O D H O H
B O L G C G G D O D D O G G O
E G S E S O E G J O G G I C U
R G G B D G B A G K O W F A S
R E O O G A W N R C D O G R E
Y D D O N G A Y H E S O O T G
Y L D E G P D O G G D D D H O
G Y D O G F I S H D O G G O D
L E R E G G O D O G W A T C H
```

◊ DOGBANE

◊ DOGBERRY

◊ DOGCART

◊ DOGCATCHER

◊ DOGDOM

◊ DOGEARED

◊ DOGFIGHT

◊ DOGFISH

◊ DOGGEDLY

◊ DOGGEDNESS

◊ DOGGEREL

◊ DOGGISHLY

◊ DOGGONE

◊ DOGHOUSE

◊ DOGLEG

◊ DOGMATIC

◊ DOGNAP

◊ DOGSBODY

◊ DOGSLEDDING

◊ DOGVANE

◊ DOGWATCH

◊ DOGWOOD

```
A H T R A M B F L O W Y R C A
F Y P B P L G E T W K I B R T
W C R N U S A H O R G R A O O
W G S E V R I R B O A E I U M
L B P H U P H C D P D T O A I
Y S U D E T W L K L C N R D C
A K W T A W L M N R O I E S I
R V A J T U O V W I A W P J Y
T A N I B E D L U H V D N A M
S U N Y V D R H F K B I U W S
E C A O R O Y F G B O M G N Y
A B L A C G C W L T V P A R A
M W O D H S N A C Y T M E T D
U F H N W P C U I U E V L H S
S U M O E K R O H H O U N D C
```

◊ *ATOMIC DOG*

◊ *BLACK DOG*

◊ *CRY WOLF*

◊ *DOG AND BUTTERFLY*

◊ *DOG DAYS ARE OVER*

◊ *DOGS IN MIDWINTER*

◊ *GIVIN' THE DOG A BONE*

◊ *HAIR OF THE DOG*

◊ *HEY BULLDOG*

◊ *HOUND DOG*

◊ *HOUNDS OF LOVE*

◊ *HUNGRY LIKE THE WOLF*

◊ *I WANNA BE YOUR DOG*

◊ *I'LL NAME THE DOGS*

◊ *MARTHA MY DEAR*

◊ *OLD BLUE*

◊ *SEAMUS THE DOG*

◊ *SHE WOLF*

◊ *SICK AS A DOG*

◊ *STRAY DOG*

◊ *THROW THE DOG A BONE*

◊ *WHO LET THE DOGS OUT*

```
S N R A E G W Y L D N E I R F
F A M I L Y N S N R E T T A P
N C O M P A R I S O N N V J S
F S T R O N G Y G W B C A U B
T R E L A N T S E G R A L D R
R C N R R A T H E R O P T D E
E U J K I N D L U W A J Y E E
M T O H L U P O N T D N T U D
O S Y E C I Q E I E A R G T N
N B E A T E R E R M O N R S A
S A H L L S N B R H I S E C L
I K U T B T E E S K I D A H E
M M N H P O G W I Z A J T E M
D E T Y I M N H E T A O C S O
G R E K I N O M E N O U G H H
```

Group: Working

Background: Bred in Germany, the name Great Dane is somewhat a misnomer, and indeed in their homeland they are referred to as the Deutsche dogge. Originally bred to join nobles on the hunt, they now make an excellent family pet.

Description: One of the largest domestic breeds, the Great Dane is muscular and strong and cuts a rather impressive figure. The breed has a broad muzzle and an alert appearance with a short coat in a number of patterns.

Temperament: A kind, friendly, and patient breed, the temperament of the Great Dane in comparison to its size frequently earns it the moniker of "gentle giant".

Energy Level: Though a sedate breed this large dog requires multiple walks per day to stay fit and healthy. Once old enough they'll enjoy joining their owners jogging and hiking.

```
P H V X X B N F R U S S E L L
I D N U O H Y E R G H P U E W
T C H I T F I V D E F R L O E
B A E O S B Z J T L U I A P I
U T T G A Z E L M N O N W A M
L A U S T R A L I A N G N R A
L H M Q Y N A A G S Q E A D R
R O A B D Y B H P I H R I E A
O U L X E I N E P B A H T P N
D L A R H A B I E E E N A D E
A A M S M O G L D R K B M E R
R S X R X R Y L V I Z S L A M
B B E E B N E O E A I E A O O
A G R L E N W C V N L I D Q V
L E L D O O P E L A D E R I A
```

◊ **AIREDALE TERRIER**

◊ **AUSTRALIAN SHEPHERD**

◊ **BEAGLE**

◊ **BELGIAN SHEPHERD**

◊ **BORDER COLLIE**

◊ **BOXER**

◊ **CATAHOULA LEOPARD DOG**

◊ **DALMATIAN**

◊ **FOX TERRIER**

◊ **GERMAN SHEPHERD**

◊ **GOLDEN RETRIEVER**

◊ **GREYHOUND**

◊ **JACK RUSSELL**

◊ **LABRADOR**

◊ **MALAMUTE**

◊ **PHARAOH HOUND**

◊ **PIT BULL**

◊ **POODLE**

◊ **SHETLAND SHEEPDOG**

◊ **SHIBA INU**

◊ **SIBERIAN HUSKY**

◊ **SPRINGER SPANIEL**

◊ **VIZSLA**

◊ **WEIMARANER**

Excerpt from *A Popular Personage At Home* by Thomas Hardy

"I live here: 'Wessex' is my name:

I am a dog known rather well:

I guard the house but how that came

To be my whim I cannot tell.

"With a leap and a heart elate I go

At the end of an hour's expectancy

To take a walk of a mile or so

With the folk I let live here with me.

"Along the path, amid the grass

I sniff, and find out rarest smells

For rolling over as I pass

The open fields toward the dells.

"No doubt I shall always cross this sill,

And turn the corner, and stand steady,

Gazing back for my Mistress till

She reaches where I have run already..."

```
R E N R O C N A M E S U O H E
S E H C A E R T O W A R D P R
H T A P S S E R T S I M I L E
R B R H T K P U M H A P I I H
H U U E L S R E O D P Y A H W
N O A A N N L U Y U C R T S W
R D W I P L R D D N I A W T S
Y O F E S S E L A T E R E F Y
O F L K L O F T E V R E S I A
G V D L K N C C R O S S E W
A M E N I E V I L E A T E L L
Z D O R P N K E A R R L X D A
I W F X E A G A G O D E O S L
N D E M A C E K T R A E H N Y
G U A R D R O L R E H T A R G
```

Popular Breed Profile: Yorkshire Terrier

```
L D N A L G N E L L U K S T Y
E S M A L L T S A N R P K E D
T D H R E D R O S T A T U R E
A J E Y B E E N O R T H E R N
N L C T N L L H K G N O L I S
O H E I I A A L E B S U C E D
I A M V H R I C E A E G H R E
T P Y I E N I N K B R H G M R
C P H T G L E P R L I T O O U
E Y T C O A S E S A U H D D F
F F L A T T E N E D Q J P E F
F T A H P D Y T S I E F A R I
A A E M A C E B S E R U L A O
I O H U M B L E U S T O U T C
U C W E V I C T O R I A N E T
```

Group: Toy

Background: Though it had humble beginnings as the dog of miners in the northern counties of England, this breed became a popular lapdog for ladies during the Victorian era.

Description: A small toy terrier with a long coat. They have a small, slightly flattened skull, dark sparkling eyes, and a black nose.

Temperament: This breed is spirited, affectionate, and alert. Though small in stature it is stout of heart with a feisty personality beneath its coiffured coat.

Energy Level: This small breed still requires moderate levels of activity in order to stay healthy but is happy in an apartment home.

```
R Y T U V G P E O P L E A R N
G A H T E C N A D V O R S S E
C B E A K D B I R S E T Y O A
M H C R E W C R S G N O S C H
T B A B S H A Q U A T V T K S
E A T S E L U L L S H P S S A
A R A W E I A P K F H C O K W
S K I A R R E D E I E S P C C
E N V R L S G M N H N E E E R
G E E Y U N N D A I L G T R E
S L J O I T N F I H F A W A
S V H C S A T F E E L E G O T
M E E R F R I D G E U M B K I
E L U T J N B N O O L L A B N
Y B G M G S R A C I J N D N G
```

◊ STOP <u>SNIFFING</u> <u>GATEPOSTS</u>

◊ <u>BRUSH</u> TEETH <u>REGULARLY</u>

◊ DON'T <u>BURST</u> A KID'S <u>BALLOON</u>

◊ DON'T <u>BARK</u> AT <u>THE TV</u>

◊ DON'T <u>CHASE</u> CARS

◊ <u>LEARN</u> TO ASK <u>NICELY</u>

◊ STOP <u>CHASING</u> <u>SQUIRRELS</u>

◊ DON'T <u>WRECK</u> THE CAT'S <u>BED</u>

◊ DON'T <u>WASH</u> YOUR <u>REAR</u> END WHEN <u>PEOPLE</u> ARE <u>EATING</u>

◊ DON'T <u>PEE</u> ON <u>THE CAT</u>

◊ STOP <u>CHEWING</u> PENS

◊ DON'T PUSH <u>TOYS</u> <u>BEHIND</u> THE <u>FRIDGE</u>

◊ STOP BITING THE <u>LEAVES</u> OF <u>HOUSEPLANTS</u>

◊ DON'T <u>DANCE</u> AROUND A HUMAN'S <u>FEET</u> WHEN THEY ARE <u>WALKING</u>

◊ DON'T <u>TEASE</u> THE <u>MAILMAN</u>

◊ <u>STOP</u> HIDING <u>SOCKS</u>

```
D N A I N A R E M O P S B E P
J E Y E D N U H S H C A D S U
E T D F R R L E U O S E B E S
U B D R V K O I T S S P A G D
E L R S A O T T E R H O U N D
P O O D L E I T T U F N V I E
K O E C H S B V S W J L E K Y
N D S S H D U K B G E R S E O
O H E H E I Y N L N I I L P M
F O T E C L H X I H N G L C A
F U L P A S O U S A A O F E S
I N A H I F N K A E B P A K R
R D M E R Y R N B H E I C N V
G A R R N O A K S J U F H T H
N H T D Y C A L A S K A N S U
```

◊ ALASKAN MALAMUTE

◊ BASSET HOUND

◊ BEAGLE

◊ BEARDED COLLIE

◊ BLOODHOUND

◊ BRUSSELS GRIFFON

◊ CAIRN TERRIER

◊ CANAAN DOG

◊ CHIHUAHUA

◊ DACHSHUND

◊ FOX TERRIER

◊ GERMAN SHEPHERD

◊ MALTESE

◊ OTTERHOUND

◊ PEKINGESE

◊ POMERANIAN

◊ POODLE

◊ RAT TERRIER

◊ ROTTWEILER

◊ SAMOYED

◊ SCOTTISH TERRIER

◊ SHIBA INU

◊ SIBERIAN HUSKY

◊ YORKSHIRE TERRIER

```
D R E S L K C A B E G D I R C
B E R G E R T H O S T Y N A B
K A I K E N V M V Y T T T E J
D N U H L L A V K E O A M S W
A N E D K E A S R C L E Z T L
D N O R C C I K U G S P I E N
I A S A E E I R O R Y O P L D
E I I W R C U D O M H D S A E
C V N A D N U C N K O E A U H
A U G V D E E A S I R N L J U
N R I O N N U N E K C G D U N
A E N H A V L Y C B H O I O D
A P G C E K R E P P I H C S R
N S A L U K I O R J D L J O I
```

◊ BEAUCERON

◊ BERGER PICARD

◊ CANAAN DOG

◊ CANE CORSO

◊ CATALBURUN

◊ CESKY TERRIER

◊ DANDIE DINMONT TERRIER

◊ ESTRELA MOUNTAIN DOG

◊ FINNISH SPITZ

◊ HOVAWART

◊ KAI KEN

◊ KOMONDOR

◊ NEW GUINEA SINGING DOG

◊ NORWEGIAN LUNDEHUND

◊ PERUVIAN INCA ORCHID

◊ PLOTT HOUND

◊ PORTUGUESE PODENGO

◊ SALUKI

◊ SCHIPPERKE

◊ THAI RIDGEBACK

◊ SWEDISH VALLHUND

```
D G N I T A E B A R C P T W C
A E D D F C O Y O T E F E R S
R V S F Y H E A L T I L L A A
W D D H Y O U H I W L Y C W P
I N B R O A A K S A F I M L M
N A V U C R N O K B T K A W A
S I K F S Y T C E C M G N T P
N P C N B H A E R P N W E C F
K O U D A J D A A E L E D E G
D I O Y I R K O B R I U N D O
N H U C D P U Y G C E N C G L
A T O S C E A H H R E D J C D
L E U L P A D L C C V P U P E
S N B A E V R H E E D E N F N
I P C V J E S C O R S A C M C
```

◊ AFRICAN GOLDEN WOLF

◊ ARCTIC FOX

◊ BENGAL FOX

◊ BUSH DOG

◊ CAPE FOX

◊ CORSAC FOX

◊ COYOTE

◊ CRAB-EATING FOX

◊ CULPEO

◊ DARWIN'S FOX

◊ DHOLE

◊ ETHIOPIAN WOLF

◊ FENNEC FOX

◊ GOLDEN JACKAL

◊ HOARY FOX

◊ ISLAND FOX

◊ KIT FOX

◊ MANED WOLF

◊ PALE FOX

◊ PAMPAS FOX

◊ RACCOON DOG

◊ SECHURAN FOX

◊ SHORT-EARED DOG

◊ SWIFT FOX

```
S Y R I A H L U A W R E T A C
O K T V K Y H E R C U L E S F
S R C H G N G A Z R P S S F Y
K S Z I G V I S Y T O W T J Y
R D R A R I S L C W I G V S K
O S E N C T T A A A T N T I K
W C T G S H O O M M R T H N O
T A S K T N A A G T O F C C T
E T N G T U D R R P S A A G S
K T O F U Y R W Y S P I E C R
S E M U F F I N B E L K R O E
A R I A T N B Y R K I I O H J
B C N H Y R A L C A M D N L C
A A I C R A C K E R S F T K B
I T M V E N O B L I T Z E R Y
```

◊ *BLITZER MALONEY*

◊ *BOTTOMLEY POTTS*

◊ *HAIRY MACLARY SCATTERCAT*

◊ *HAIRY MACLARY, SHOO*

◊ *HAIRY MACLARY, SIT*

◊ *HAIRY MACLARY'S BONE*

◊ *HAIRY MACLARY'S CATERWAUL CAPER*

◊ *HAIRY MACLARY'S HAT TRICKS*

◊ *HERCULES MORSE*

◊ *MUFFIN MCLAY*

◊ *SCARFACE CLAW, HOLD TIGHT*

◊ *SCHNITZEL VON KRUMM'S BASKETWORK*

◊ *SLINKY MALINKI EARLY BIRD*

◊ *SLINKY MALINKI OPEN THE DOOR*

◊ *SLINKY MALINKI'S CHRISTMAS CRACKERS*

◊ *ZACHARY QUACK MINIMONSTER*

Excerpt from *Three Men in a Boat (To Say Nothing of the Dog)* by Jerome K. Jerome

To look at Montmorency you would imagine that he was an angel sent upon the earth, for some reason withheld from mankind, in the shape of a small fox-terrier. There is a sort of Oh-what-a-wicked-world-this-is-and-how-I-wish-I-could-do-something-to-make-it-better-and-nobler expression about Montmorency that has been known to bring the tears into the eyes of pious old ladies and gentlemen.

When first he came to live at my expense, I never thought I should be able to get him to stop long. I used to sit down and look at him, as he sat on the rug and looked up at me, and think: "Oh, that dog will never live. He will be snatched up to the bright skies in a chariot, that is what will happen to him."

But, when I had paid for about a dozen chickens that he had killed; and had dragged him, growling and kicking, by the scruff of his neck, out of a hundred and fourteen street fights; and had had a dead cat brought round for my inspection by an irate female, who called me a murderer; and had been summoned by the man next door but one for having a ferocious dog at large, that had kept him pinned up in his own tool-shed, afraid to venture his nose outside the door for over two hours on a cold night; and had learned that the gardener, unknown to myself, had won thirty shillings by backing him to kill rats against time, then I began to think that maybe they'd let him remain on earth for a bit longer, after all.

```
D E L L I K H S E R U T N E V
N M S R A E T T Y T R I H T K
O L O N G E R A R N E H T F G
I U N N E V E R E A N I H E R
S S E M T P B U T G E T O R O
S N P U U M X D A E D S U O W
E A P T D R O E R B R R G C L
R T A E E F D R I A A I H I I
P C H E K F E E E N G F T O N
X H E R O U N D R N I G C U G
E E L T O R N D D E C G E S V
R D B S L C I O M O R Y H D P
U N A M S S P Z P I O U S T O
G R E A S O N E C H A R I O T
L A D I E S G N I A M E R K S
```

101

```
D M C I T E N E G O D A L C S
O N A C Y L G O D I T P E P D
G H S R S H E E P D O G F G E
W V K U G E D D O G S O O G G
H A H D O O M A R G O D N O G
G G T S U N D O G K P L E D O
B O O E A T E A H A D L G H D
G G D D R M N G L A C U O C D
O P O A R D I J O C N B D T R
D V G D E E O D H D H G E A I
P I E N L S D G O O N U D W B
H P A R G O D N O G T E F O U
A W K T D J L W U H E D O D G
B O O N D O G G L E P N O O O
A N T I D O G M A T I C S G D
```

◊ AMIDOGENS

◊ ANTIDOGMATIC

◊ BIRDDOGGED

◊ BOONDOGGLE

◊ BULLDOG

◊ CLADO-
  GENETIC

◊ CLADOGRAM

◊ ENDOGENOUS

◊ HANGDOG

◊ HOTDOG

◊ LAPDOG

◊ ONDOGRAM

◊ ONDOGRAPH

◊ OVERDOG

◊ PEPTI-
  DOGLYCAN

◊ SEADOG

◊ SHEEPDOG

◊ SUNDOG

◊ UNDERDOG

◊ WATCHDOG

◊ WATERDOG

Group: Non-sporting/Toy

Background: Believed to have originated in Tenerife as early as the 13th or 14th century, making their way to mainland Europe with traders and becoming popular with nobility.

Description: With a name that means "white dog", it is unsurprising that the bichon is known for its distinct plush, white, corkscrew-curled, hypoallergenic coat that just invites attention.

Temperament: A friendly, happy, lively, and outgoing breed. As a companion breed they do well with children and other pets and are obedient if well-trained. They can become territorial.

Energy Level: Characterized by bursts of energy with long moments of calm, this small breed is happy with a daily walk and play.

Name Ideas for White Dogs

```
D F F U P R E D W O P Y S R L
L J J E D A Y Y O O T T T T A
G A A F A O D J I O F S S G P
G R R N J I V M L S B I O O O
L H G S A J E E G I M M V H Y
G E B M A R S H M A L L O W G
L P O L A R B E A R V Y O G E
E N U V F Y E B E M H N S R H
D A R H W S C D W C S W U V C
F K T W E I N L R L O Y G L N
R S A M Y A N Y O N N R A O A
O A D Y E D S T N U U B R K L
S L N L G T J U E E D O R P B
T A O G A J A Y W R W P L I Y
Y S N L D I H C R O L G V C E
```

◊ ALASKA

◊ ANGEL

◊ BLANCHE

◊ BOO

◊ BRIE

◊ CLOUD

◊ CRYSTAL

◊ DAISY

◊ DIAMOND

◊ DOVE

◊ FROSTY

◊ GHOST

◊ GWEN

◊ LILY

◊ MARSH-
   MALLOW

◊ MISTY

◊ OLEANDER

◊ OPAL

◊ ORCHID

◊ PEARL

◊ POLAR BEAR

◊ POWDER PUFF

◊ SNOWY

◊ SUGAR

◊ WINTER

```
E K I P S M V N S Y O M M F U
F R I E D A S F E O N T A J S
I K D N A L E L R M P L M U M
N L Y D I A L K Y A O H N I M
U J O S O O N C A Y N I I F R
R H E S V K H O U B L K C E L
E N T E C D M T R U F F L E S
R I A O M H A S I R Y C A I P
E K G H K T R D N A C S R L N
U P A P S H C O U O E T A L E
D M E N I H I O E L O E I L B
O U O G U G E W B D C P L A R
R P J F G J P R N T E E Y G O
A N F H D Y A E M F B R C F W
U P N N Y M A C N Y L L A S N
```

- ◊ BELLE
- ◊ CHARLIE BROWN
- ◊ CLARA
- ◊ EUDORA
- ◊ FRANKLIN
- ◊ FRIEDA
- ◊ GREAT PUMPKIN
- ◊ JOE AGATE

- ◊ LELAND
- ◊ LINUS
- ◊ LYDIA
- ◊ MARBLES
- ◊ MARCIE
- ◊ MOLLY VOLLEY
- ◊ OLAF
- ◊ PEGGY JEAN
- ◊ PIG-PEN
- ◊ RERUN

- ◊ RUBY
- ◊ SALLY BROWN
- ◊ SCHROEDER
- ◊ SHERMY
- ◊ SNOOPY
- ◊ SOPHIE
- ◊ SPIKE
- ◊ TRUFFLES
- ◊ WOODSTOCK

```
P P E L T U Y C F K G R M B N
M S M A U H S S T O R M R E K
O E S U S B T Y H C A L A M I
B B K I T G R M L M S J G N R
R R O T M S E L I B J N O P B
Y O F Y L C B E N S M S S E Y
I H C H K E O M U I E A C W Y
B S S K J C R F K E E D S Y Y
B O L A I L U E T J L I S R I
S J M K M R M H E K R E O R E
K E I C G A H W C E A K U E E
S N D V B J N R E A C M I F L
G W Y I R Y L T B I O V I C E
L T S P O S L W H R T I O K E
F P G N N Y L F T A E L L T L
```

◊ CARLEE   ◊ KING   ◊ ROCKI

◊ CHUCKY   ◊ KIRBY   ◊ RUFUS

◊ FERRY   ◊ LEE LEE   ◊ RUMOR

◊ FLYNN   ◊ MALACHY   ◊ SADIE

◊ HICKORY   ◊ MAMIE   ◊ SAMANTHA

◊ JAMES   ◊ MIKE   ◊ SIBA

◊ JOEY   ◊ MISS P   ◊ STORM

◊ JOSH   ◊ ROBERT   ◊ STUMP

```
Y X A M M I M I R A C L E K W
N O P D Y E L N A T S Q N S O
A N G C O J R H I S T O R Y H
C K Y R I G N L O O W S H K E
S L O E E E D P E S S U H C R
U D V P N T H A L S C I Y U O
T O G O B I T I Y K B G S L E
L I K F E S T E B S O A E N S
E O N O T T R N B O K B B N P
I T O S L Q A A I K R E D S E
D Y I E I A Q H U T O N D Y A
O H T R K D L P W D N B A R K
B D U B P D E Q O F I I O J E
G E N I U S T T B P O I R P Z
P S Y L L U F H T I A F R K Z
```

◇ A BIG <u>LITTLE</u> LIFE

◇ <u>BODIE</u> ON THE <u>ROAD</u>

◇ <u>BORN</u> TO <u>BARK</u>

◇ <u>DOG DAYS</u> OF <u>HISTORY</u>

◇ DOG <u>HEROES</u>

◇ <u>FAITHFULLY</u> YOURS

◇ FINDING <u>GOBI</u>

◇ HOW DOGS <u>LOVE</u> US

◇ HOW TO <u>SPEAK</u> DOG

◇ <u>HUCK</u>

◇ <u>INSIDE</u> OF A DOG

◇ <u>LUCKY</u> FOR ME

◇ <u>MAX THE</u> <u>MIRACLE</u> DOG

◇ <u>MERLE'S</u> DOG

◇ NO <u>BETTER</u> FRIEND

◇ <u>OOGY</u>

◇ <u>PUKKA'S</u> <u>PROMISE</u>

◇ <u>RESCUING</u> <u>SPRITE</u>

◇ <u>RIN TIN TIN</u>

◇ <u>STANLEY</u> AND <u>SOPHIE</u>

◇ THE <u>GENIUS</u> OF DOGS

◇ <u>TODO IN</u> <u>TUSCANY</u>

◇ <u>WHAT THE DOG</u> <u>KNOWS</u>

In North Wales, the village of Beddgelert is much visited for its most famous historical feature: Gelert's Grave. Sadly, although Prince Llewelyn did exist, the dog is almost certainly the invention of David Pritchard, landlord of the Royal Goat Inn, whose aim was to increase trade at the inn. He and other villagers erected a tombstone, the story on which reads:

In the 13th <u>century</u> Llewelyn <u>Prince</u> of <u>North</u> <u>Wales</u> had a <u>palace</u> at Beddgelert. One day he went <u>hunting</u> without Gelert "The <u>Faithful</u> <u>Hound</u>" who was unaccountably <u>absent</u>.

On Llewelyn's return, the <u>truant</u> <u>stained</u> and smeared <u>with</u> blood joyfully <u>sprang</u> to meet his <u>master</u>. The prince alarmed hastened to <u>find</u> his <u>son</u> and saw the <u>infant's</u> <u>cot</u> <u>empty</u>, the bedclothes and <u>floor</u> covered with <u>blood</u>.

The <u>frantic</u> father plunged his <u>sword</u> into the hound's <u>side</u> thinking it had <u>killed</u> his <u>heir</u>. The dog's <u>dying</u> <u>yell</u> was answered by a <u>child's</u> <u>cry</u>.

Llewelyn <u>searched</u> and discovered his <u>boy</u> unharmed but <u>near</u> by lay the <u>body</u> of a <u>mighty</u> <u>wolf</u> which Gelert had <u>slain</u>. The prince filled with <u>remorse</u> is said never to have <u>smiled</u> again. He <u>buried</u> Gelert here.

The spot is called

<u>BEDDGELERT</u>

```
W H L U F H T I A F K R A E N
D T R C O G N A C H I L D S S
E I W U N F Y Y B R L N T W L
L W N A A F R E O S L R O R J
I D R N L A C O L B E R R E C
M P T O B E L B G L D N C I E
S S W R L F S D E N I A T S O
L G M T O T R G S R L N R U D
L N I H O P D E E A A O T E N
E I G C D D A T P R M R I I G
W T H N E R S R F E U R A Y N
E N T B C A I S R A U L D T I
L U Y H M N D E N B S O N P Y
Y H E E C U E T H H B M I M D
N D R E Y R U T N E C A F E J
```

Unusual Breed Profile: Bergamasco Sheepdog

```
N I A T N U O M U S C U L A R
T A L P I N E R N M E O S B M
I N O I N A P M O C V Y T C O
I E E A E V I T C E T O R P D
N V R I R K D L L A M S O E E
T I E G C E D I S T U O N M R
E T N E D N E P E D N I G A A
L A W R E O A A P A T I E N T
L N O B S L A R G E T O W N E
I C A E E V I T C N I T S I D
G D Y R V O V A C T I V I T Y
E E E G V S P K Y H G U O H T
N M R A W S G I N S T I N C T
T O L M L O G N I P E E K T G
N H F O D E M G L E A S T I F
```

Group: Herding/Pastoral

Background: An ancient Italian Alpine dog taking its name from the town of Bergamo.

Description: A large and muscular dog with big, oval eyes, it is distinctive due to its corded coat, which is ideal for keeping the dog warm in its native mountain home.

Temperament: This is an intelligent and patient breed that, though independent, makes a good companion. They have a strong protective instinct.

Energy Level: Needing moderate exercise, this breed would love to spend time partaking in an activity with its owner. It requires a large home with at least a small outside space.

```
O C W O H C W O H C N O F E N
K E E S H O N D W T A A V L N
O S S P Z T I P S H K S G K A
N H W A Y F O N D U S I U H I
P I E A B I J N E S A B P O G
S B D S N P U W E K L U D U E
H A I A S H O S S Y A N E N W
A I S H L H E M I A A H E D R
R N H L N G I K E L M U S W O
P U A E N A U H N R R O E P N
E V A I E L H E T A A A Y I Z
I J K E A L E G S Z U N H E R
K E I S J R G I F P U C I P D
P A T B G L E C P A L J G A R
J W A U F R E Z U A N H C S N
```

◊ AFGHAN HOUND

◊ AKITA

◊ ALASKAN MALAMUTE

◊ BASENJI

◊ CHINESE SHAR PEI

◊ CHOW CHOW

◊ EURASIER

◊ FINNISH SPITZ

◊ GREENLAND DOG

◊ JAPANESE CHIN

◊ KEESHOND

◊ LHASA APSO

◊ NORWEGIAN ELKHOUND

◊ PEKINGESE

◊ POMERANIAN

◊ SALUKI

◊ SAMOYED

◊ SCHNAUZER

◊ SHIBA INU

◊ SHIH TZU

◊ SIBERIAN HUSKY

◊ SWEDISH VALLHUND

```
O D N F R N Y U H D W S T A V
R N B A W E U K R V C A R I N
E E I U A L Z A S O R M A R B
X A K T L N N U R U F O W R R
O G O R N R A S A F H Y A E E
B K M G E E O C I N C E V H G
L N O B R I G T E I H D O C R
E M N O K E S R T C T C H S E
O A D A N A E A A W N K S N B
B L O K M I K N R E E S E I N
R A R L U R H I L U L I D P O
E M L F D V E C T A E A L I E
O U V H I V A B K A N T F E L
B T B R H C I S O E I D M K R
S E E N E R Y P Z D N D N D K
```

◊ AKITA

◊ ALASKAN
 MALAMUTE

◊ BOERBOEL

◊ BOXER

◊ BULLMASTIFF

◊ CANAAN DOG

◊ CANE CORSO

◊ CHINOOK

◊ DOBERMANN

◊ DOGO
 ARGENTINO

◊ EURASIER

◊ GERMAN
 PINSCHER

◊ GIANT
 SCHNAUZER

◊ GREAT DANE

◊ GREAT
 PYRENEES

◊ GREENLAND
 DOG

◊ HOVAWART

◊ KOMONDOR

◊ KUVASZ

◊ LEONBERGER

◊ ROTTWEILER

◊ SAINT
 BERNARD

◊ SAMOYED

◊ SIBERIAN
 HUSKY

```
K Y O J K R T U H R V U U T P
T T N A S A F N Y V J O S U I
F R N V N O F P A A D F W O A
S I A G B O F M W C T L E R P
M N E N J L T A Y M H N E P I
U K B V E E O C I T M O T S P
R E Y V K U U S L R F T I U I
F T L C K P T E S G Y T E C P
F S I G C R A R J O L U P A P
C R T A O F A N O I M B H H I
C W K G G H O U U N I R M C N
B E G I M L I G Q C N L F L G
H H Z O A U V G R Y N P S A W
R M A P P L E E S H I S N A P
O D S V V E C T J D E O Y L D
```

◊ APPLE	◊ GIZMO	◊ QUARK
◊ BEAN	◊ GNAT	◊ SCAMP
◊ BLOSSOM	◊ LEAF	◊ SMURF
◊ BUTTON	◊ MINNIE	◊ SNAP
◊ CRICKET	◊ NACHO	◊ SPROUT
◊ CUPCAKE	◊ NEUTRON	◊ SWEETIE
◊ FAIRY	◊ NUGGET	◊ TRINKET
◊ GIMLI	◊ PIPPIN	◊ WASP

```
S N Y F J D Y K C O R Y Z L S
E I T A Y L L L B K I U K I N
T W O O W C W O L G M M C B I
U S M C B D E K R A D B N E W
C L M R N R O R W A H S A R T
K B L C P A U O U A H S K T H
E S A H C O R T G T L C R Y H
H L L A I Y R F G J N L H A E
I O H Y E U V T G M S E Y R M
A O T S E R E V E R R J V P L
Y K R Y E L B B U R Y S I D K
G O T A C D L I W N X D K K A
G U N R E K C A R T R E E O T
O T P U C R O B O D O G R R I
F A T T E L A K C I H C O M E
```

◊ ADVENTURE BAY

◊ CALI

◊ CAP'N TURBOT

◊ CHASE

◊ CHICKALETTA

◊ ELLA

◊ EVEREST

◊ FOGGY BOTTOM

◊ FRANCOIS TURBOT

◊ HAROLD HUMDINGER

◊ KATIE

◊ LIBERTY

◊ MARSHALL

◊ MAYOR GOODWAY

◊ MIGHTY TWINS

◊ MR. PORTER

◊ REX

◊ ROBO-DOG

◊ ROCKY

◊ RUBBLE

◊ RYDER

◊ SKYE

◊ THE LOOKOUT

◊ TRACKER

◊ TUCK

◊ WALLY

◊ WILD CAT

◊ ZUMA

Popular Breed Profile: Dachshund

```
R H O U S E I T E I R A V O M
A W L E C B S L I M H O U N D
L A R A R A E S O U N A L M V
U Y P E U N L R E I S O P S L
G S E S N S E E C N W R N P O
E D A E Y N U K A C H R U M Y
R G K E E L N N O S E S E P A
E S G I R A I U U T T A A N L
S T W N M U R S T A N D A R D
K S L E O A T A A S V M A B G
L E S L G R P A M E R I C A N
A G C E A O T A T E K M C D O
W G O K A M K S G S C W E G L
R U S I Z E S O C I A L S E K
S S D I S T I N C T L P S R H
```

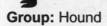

Group: Hound

Background: A breed of German origin, its name means "badger hound". As this suggests, its distinct shape allowed it to easily make its way underground in pursuit of its prey.

Description: The long and low body of the dachshund is distinctive and easily recognised, giving rise to nicknames such as wiener dog and sausage dog. There are long-haired, smooth-haired, and wire-haired varieties in both standard and miniature sizes with various patterns.

Temperament: Small in size, the dachshund more than makes up for its lack of stature in personality. Spunky, social, and loyal, the breed is described by both the American and British Kennel clubs as courageous to the point of rashness.

Energy Level: Regular, moderate length walks allow the dachshund to stay strong to support its unusual form. They are happy in a house with access to at least a small outdoor space.

Excerpt from *White Fang*
by Jack London

White Fang felt fear mounting in him again. He could not quite suppress a snarl, but he made no offer to snap. The hand, with fingers crooked and spread apart, rubbed his stomach in a playful way and rolled him from side to side. It was ridiculous and ungainly, lying there on his back with legs sprawling in the air. Besides, it was a position of such utter helplessness that White Fang's whole nature revolted against it. He could do nothing to defend himself. If this man-animal intended harm, White Fang knew that he could not escape it. How could he spring away with his four legs in the air above him? Yet submission made him master his fear, and he only growled softly. This growl he could not suppress; nor did the man-animal resent it by giving him a blow on the head. And furthermore, such was the strangeness of it, White Fang experienced an unaccountable sensation of pleasure as the hand rubbed back and forth. When he was rolled on his side he ceased to growl, when the fingers pressed and prodded at the base of his ears the pleasurable sensation increased; and when, with a final rub and scratch, the man left him alone and went away, all fear had died out of White Fang. He was to know fear many times in his dealing with man; yet it was a token of the fearless companionship with man that was ultimately to be his.

```
O L K S D G P J S R E G N I F
C A C Y T E A L B D P N E M S
E N A L A R L B E U A I K A U
X I B N K W A L O A C T O S P
P F T I M E S N O V S N T T P
E D S A S N G N G R E U T E R
R E P G C O H R A E S O R R E
I D R N R L A T O P N M I E S
E D I U A A R P R W C E U A S
N O N S T O M A C H L R S R H
C R G E C A W D E F E N D S T
E P Y B H L N A P S R U O F R
D U L T I M A T E L Y V R A O
A O I N A K O N W H I T E N F
W W G N O I T I S O P F M G J
```

```
B E R N E S E R I H S K R O Y
G I R R M O F B A S S E T M M
E E C E S H I H T Z U I I W J
C S B H H E L D O O P X E H S
O E I R O C T K E T E M M I R
P N G U I N S A B D A S T P K
A I H R N T F N W E A B W P I
P H E E E N T R I G O L D E N
I C Y I T Y A A I P W E N T G
L O W L L T H G N S N S P C G
L R B A N S T O I Y E E A N N
O G K V F K T N U D V T F G S
N I G A L S Z I V N R L F F I
A U M C O G R E A T D A N E A
P L A B R A D O R T E M C A R
```

◊ AFFEN-
   PINSCHER

◊ BASSET
   HOUND

◊ BERNESE
   MOUNTAIN DOG

◊ BICHON FRISE

◊ BOSTON
   TERRIER

◊ BRITTANY

◊ CARDIGAN
   WELSH CORGI

◊ CHINESE
   CRESTED

◊ GOLDEN
   RETRIEVER

◊ GREAT DANE

◊ GREYHOUND

◊ KING CHARLES
   CAVALIER

◊ LABRADOR
   RETRIEVER

◊ MALTESE

◊ MIXED BREED

◊ PAPILLON

◊ POODLE

◊ PUG

◊ SHIH TZU

◊ VIZSLA

◊ WHIPPET

◊ YORKSHIRE
   TERRIER

```
E E V P F D I X I E J D U V P
O F C R R P N W M M A Y T C T
C L R P A A O D M I L O Y S L
S D H E N D A N N Y P L D P N
O Y V A C T T G G Y H F A U R
R D U G O K U W R O A T I O C
D F N K I T L O B I C P L R Y
E Y L I S P D E G H M L U S H
T R S E E A U C S A Y P A A C
R O E G N T C J R Y U Y C M T
T T B P M O S T C S T M Y M A
W U B Y P A L N L A O S F A R
N L M S T O A O I O Y C U G C
L P F I I L C P C E N W A R S
M M R J J M R H M R E S W O T
```

◊ ALPHA   ◊ FRANCOIS   ◊ ROLLY

◊ BOLT   ◊ FRECKLES   ◊ ROSCOE

◊ COLONEL   ◊ GAMMA   ◊ SCRATCHY

◊ COPPER   ◊ MOOCH   ◊ SCUD

◊ DANNY   ◊ NANA   ◊ TOBY

◊ DIXIE   ◊ PATCH   ◊ TOWSER

◊ DUG   ◊ PLUTO   ◊ TRAMP

◊ EINSTEIN   ◊ PONGO   ◊ TRUSTY

◊ FLOYD   ◊ RITA

```
C B C S I A V R R G U Y I W
F N A S H O W L I D A Y F N G
C P B R N L A H I S V U J E G
J S W J K I O F F U R B A I V
Y H A U Y C F I W D L H Y L E
F C O F S K W F I L S B T L S
W A O E Y A A N E A A T W O H
B O N J G O A S E R I A K C V
W O W G V N D L N S R C E V E
B V Y P D V A R P H C E S D R
N U B A W L K A O H L H E U G
T V E M O R N W V O I L E O R
B L W N U I L H O W L I E W R
F C A F E T P I T T B U L L R
F J B L B C T O N I C W A P A
```

◊ AL PAWCINO

◊ ALEASHA KEYS

◊ ANDY WARHOWL

◊ BARK RUFFALO

◊ BILLIE HOWLIDAY

◊ BRAD PITTBULL

◊ COLLIE RINGWALD

◊ CLAUDIA SNIFFER

◊ EARTHA SITT

◊ FLEA PACE

◊ FURDINAND TORRES

◊ HOWLIE MANDEL

◊ JAMES EARL BONES

◊ JIMMY CHEW

◊ LICK OFFERMAN

◊ MUTT DAMON

◊ PETER O'DROOL

◊ RICKY GRRRVAIS

◊ SOPHIA VERGRRRA

◊ SPANIEL CRAIG

◊ VERA FANG

◊ WAGGY SMITH

◊ WOOFY HARRELSON

◊ ZACH BRUFF

Popular Breed Profile: Labrador Retriever

```
S E R I U Q E R O O D T U O L
N G H Y L D N E I R F D O O G
E D W I N T E L L I G E N T O
M S E O G N I T A N I G I R O
R R U N L H E F T E R U T A N
E E U P I L L E O O H C T A M
H M T E E F E Y R U P V B L T
S M K R C T E Y J H N S L A N
I I C H I L D R E N T D I M E
F W A F O E N G L A N D N I V
E S B H H S V N E T F O D N E
O B L A C K Y E C A N A D A R
G N I O G T U O R E D I U G P
H I S T O R Y E X E R C I S E
J V R O D A R B A L S N A E M
```

Group: Sporting/Gundog

Background: Originating in Newfoundland, Canada, the Labrador retriever was commonly found assisting fishermen. They were spotted and brought back to England where the breed was refined.

Description: A large breed usually found with one of three coats, yellow, chocolate, and black. The history of their breed means they are double-coated with webbed feet, and so are generally good swimmers.

Temperament: This friendly, outgoing, and intelligent dog is a popular choice as both a pet and a working animal. It has a good-tempered nature with children and is often seen working as a guide dog for the blind.

Energy Level: This highly energetic breed requires lots of exercise to prevent destructive tendencies. The Labrador retriever requires a large home with outdoor space to match.

```
D N E I S H I B A I N U E Q F
E A D N U O H D O O L B T Y T
T I A N A I L A R T S U A A S
U R L K D L T J X Y K K R I V
M E M F V R E D R O B E Y R W
A B A A E E A T B C N S E E O
L I T E L J I N O A I L R D H
A S I G A B Z O R O I A P A C
M N A Z E Z N A N E G G W L W
G E N T D H M I W E B P Q E O
B Z A X O I L T R A S T V R H
J N S U E A T M K T H S S L C
P Q N W M O A I A E C O R S O
B D Q M R N T I E P R A H S P
B U L L M A S T I F F X R N L
```

◇ AIREDALE TERRIER

◇ AKITA

◇ ALASKAN MALAMUTE

◇ AUSTRALIAN CATTLE DOG

◇ BEAGLE

◇ BELGIAN MALINOIS

◇ BLOODHOUND

◇ BORDER COLLIE

◇ BULLMASTIFF

◇ CANE CORSO

◇ CHOW CHOW

◇ DALMATIAN

◇ GERMAN SHEPHERD

◇ ROTTWEILER

◇ SHAR-PEI

◇ SHIBA INU

◇ SIBERIAN HUSKY

◇ SKYE TERRIER

◇ ST. BERNARD

◇ TIBETAN MASTIFF

◇ TREEING WALKER COONHOUND

◇ WEIMARANER

Name Ideas for Big Dogs – Part Two

```
A P E B N O M B Y H R L G D B
H Y N A C Y L U M Y E T I E H
P E B S W X K L T R T J E J E
L L K K R B O R O T I T A N R
A T I E G A D N W P H D H U C
C N D R G U A P K O A C N V U
J E E V S L E R V N K A G S L
Y B E I H I Y E A U S N C I E
G F K L T H N Z H A L O U K S
Y N K L P S R O L S O C E H O
F C A E L A A T D B N I A J C
S R Z T T U A B Y A K A U N Y
S A M P S O N D R E H C B U O
B L Y M L U O R E T I P U J M
S V F Y R O M C A R E N A T I
```

◊ ADONIS	◊ BENTLEY	◊ MUSTANG
◊ ALPHA	◊ CHUNK	◊ SAMPSON
◊ APOLLO	◊ CUJO	◊ SCOOBY-DOO
◊ ATLAS	◊ HERCULES	◊ TARZAN
◊ BANSHEE	◊ JUPITER	◊ TITAN
◊ BASKERVILLE	◊ KNOX	◊ VULCAN
◊ BASTIEN	◊ KODA	◊ YETI
◊ BEETHOVEN	◊ LYCAN	◊ ZEPHYR

A little Dog that wags his tail
by Emily Dickinson

A little Dog that wags his tail
And knows no other joy
Of such a little Dog am I
Reminded by a Boy

Who gambols all the living Day
Without an earthly cause
Because he is a little Boy
I honestly suppose —

The Cat that in the Corner dwells
Her martial Day forgot
The Mouse but a Tradition now
Of her desireless Lot

Another class remind me
Who neither please nor play
But not to make a "bit of noise"
Beseech each little Boy —

```
E Y G F Y C K N R G E T A I L
N S I O L O E W N E C S D J B
E L I A D I J I A B N E U E Y
L V S O T H V F E G S R C O J
T S V H N I O S S I S A O B M
T T E M L R E U R S U C H C S
I R Y R G E P E R S E O O L R
L A L O C P L L E D K C O R E
T D T H O E A A E M A B Y M H
U I S S M Y D A A M P S V T
O T E S C J N R W A S W P P O
H I N A I I T G G E O E B F N
T O O M M I D E B N L V C O A
I N H E A B U T K G O L D A Y
W S R L E A R T H L Y S S A T
```

```
E S O P R U P D U I L S N C M
D E W J I J U E D C J O S S A
J U N J U B K Y Y R B N O R R
H H M O R C A D B S V B E C M
I V E I O R W I S E D L L B A
E R A A T D G P I O L J D L D
V W O S R R Y G Y E L R A M U
O Y E N E T H B Y O Y Y L S K
L H U D W T L D O G G Y M H E
T L O B B I L T G O J O A I L
S R P E U O L A U A C C T L S
U L L W E N H L D L H S I O I
M O K S Y S P D G I I U A H F
W G O D R E N E I W N P N F E
M F W F P P B A L T O P S Y P
```

◇ *101 DALMATIANS*

◇ *A DOG'S PURPOSE*

◇ *AIR BUD*

◇ *BALTO*

◇ *BENJI*

◇ *BIG RED*

◇ *BOLT*

◇ *CUJO*

◇ *EIGHT BELOW*

◇ *HACHI*

◇ *HEART OF A DOG*

◇ *IRON WILL*

◇ *ISLE OF DOGS*

◇ *MARLEY AND ME*

◇ *MARMADUKE*

◇ *MUST LOVE DOGS*

◇ *MY DOG TULIP*

◇ *OLD YELLER*

◇ *SCOOBY-DOO*

◇ *SHILOH*

◇ *THE SHAGGY DOG*

◇ *THE STRAY*

◇ *TOGO*

◇ *WIENER-DOG*

```
F O X L I K E C I T E L H T A
G N I K R O W O I Y L E V I L
A I R E H T H P I D E M O N D
L N A T U R E A E G R A L E I
T S E I P P A H N I M S T M T
T C F V B U Y I C E S S P D N
C E I A I K O I D N E R E T E
E N L T S G M I E R E V A S G
T T M U T E C D E S A O I A I
O U H U D I R T S S C C E K L
R R O I N A N I G L R I L S L
P I P E G I V O U E A T B A E
J E S E Y E D I X Q U Y U L T
O S S T N E M E L E E P O A N
B V B A I R E B I S V R D L I
```

Group: Working

Background: Selectively bred in Siberia over centuries for their sled-pulling capabilities. This impressive breed saved the city of Nome, Alaska, from a diphtheria epidemic by delivering much-needed medicine. One of the dogs responsible, Balto, is now immortalized in film.

Description: A medium-sized dog with a double layered coat to protect it from the elements, a somewhat fox-like face with almond-shaped eyes, and an interested expression.

Temperament: The Siberian husky is an outgoing, loyal, and intelligent dog. Its working nature means it is happiest when given a job to do.

Energy Level: An athletic and lively dog, the Siberian husky requires a lot of exercise and a large home and garden.

Name Ideas for Dogs With Spots

```
O W S O I R Y L O L H C G D Y
P U O N G A V R Y N P A N D A
N W A F H N T F T V I W V O P
C S E T C P O S S S M M G C W
A H E I N A E P U B E A O U V
F B E L T I Y R D R R P C D H
R S Y E B T U G D L L H A C S
E W S E T B O Q U I E E A T L
C E R C L A E D E S T H E E H
K O E H Y S H P S L C A D I C
L S E L K N I R P S R R H P T
E Y G B G Y W A R L J A S G A
S T O D A K L O P K T B H A P
C H E C K E R S E L B R A M U
E G D U M S S N O T T U B A Y
```

◊ BUTTONS	◊ FRECKLES	◊ PEBBLES
◊ CHECKERS	◊ HARLEQUIN	◊ PERDITA
◊ CHEETAH	◊ MAGPIE	◊ POLKA DOT
◊ CHESS	◊ MARBLES	◊ PONGO
◊ DOMINO	◊ MERLE	◊ RORSCHACH
◊ DOTTIE	◊ PAISLEY	◊ SMUDGE
◊ DUSTY	◊ PANDA	◊ SPRINKLES
◊ FAWN	◊ PATCH	◊ TAPESTRY

```
V L T V S N B Z E F R Y G D F
F E A K I T A X S K E N R P F
P O D G X A B B E U G A E Y I
B B T O N W D S N V R K A R T
E R W C G A C I R A E S T E S
R E E O K O K S E S B A D N A
N O M A T O I C B Z N L A E M
A B E R G A M A S C O A N E L
R E X O B I Y O K N E R E S L
D D E E R H O U N D L H V Z U
C E R I D N U O H D O O L B B
A O S B Q W A N A T O L I A N
B H R O T T W E I L E R X O U
P I N S C H E R U S S I A N Z
N E W F O U N D L A N D T H B
```

◊ AKITA

◊ ALASKAN MALAMUTE

◊ ANATOLIAN SHEPHERD

◊ BERGAMASCO

◊ BERNESE MOUNTAIN DOG

◊ BLACK RUSSIAN TERRIER

◊ BLOODHOUND

◊ BOERBOEL

◊ BOXER

◊ BULLMASTIFF

◊ CANE CORSO

◊ DOBERMAN PINSCHER

◊ DOGO ARGENTINO

◊ GREAT DANE

◊ GREAT PYRENEES

◊ IRISH WOLFHOUND

◊ KANGAL DOG

◊ KOMONDOR

◊ KUVASZ

◊ LEONBERGER

◊ NEWFOUND-LAND

◊ ROTTWEILER

◊ SAINT BERNARD

◊ SCOTTISH DEERHOUND

Animated Dogs – Part Two

```
K A E G N E K A D Q M O T R L
L Q U A K E N V T M L V J L V
S D B U C I I U A I M A A D D
B P I F E S T H A K D B D A U
T B A L T O S E C A W R Y Y R
E I N R T G S C G O L H E E S
T D M C K D C B N D O P P P E
T O O O H Y O S G F I P H C Y
E U Q D R O O P Y D O G B A M
Y G P O I G B Y C C D N E R O
A A Y C J E Y U I U X J N N U
F L Z W B I D U K I P P E R R
A M F L O G O E M U T T L E Y
L H U J M N O F K F U T M G E
R E V I L O S C G D V B X M L
```

◊ ALPHA	◊ GIDGET	◊ PERDITA
◊ BALTO	◊ GROMIT	◊ POOCHIE
◊ BLUE	◊ KIPPER	◊ REN
◊ COPPER	◊ LADY	◊ SCOOBY-DOO
◊ DOUGAL	◊ LAFAYETTE	◊ SEYMOUR
◊ DROOPY DOG	◊ MUTTLEY	◊ SNOWBALL
◊ DUG	◊ ODIE	◊ SNOWY
◊ DUKE	◊ OLIVER	◊ SPARKY

```
C Q I O C E N R I C B A G U D
O U S L T E R R I E R O E I N
R A D N U H S H C A D O J B O
G A W H I P P E T L U E D V H
I I S L O S D K L E J R N M S
I L P O H C P U Y E W E O K E
T E D O O C B K K I A Z H U E
N L P L J E S V T J B U R W K
E D L R C T B V R G T A E S I
B I S P A N I E L A S N K P J
E S S V H H T F A I D H I I N
Y K S E C F S S E G X C O T E
O D N I J G F R R O L S O Z S
T E B R A B V H F C P E K L A
K S D O L U N I A B I H S M B
```

◊ BARBET

◊ BASENJI

◊ BEAGLE

◊ BORDER COLLIE

◊ BULLDOG

◊ BULL TERRIER

◊ CESKY TERRIER

◊ CIRNECO DELL'ETNA

◊ CORGI

◊ DACHSHUND

◊ EURASIER

◊ FINNISH SPITZ

◊ FOX TERRIER

◊ HUNGARIAN PULI

◊ KEESHOND

◊ KOOIKER-HONDJE

◊ KOREAN JINDO

◊ MINIATURE POODLE

◊ SCHNAUZER

◊ SHAR PEI

◊ SHIBA INU

◊ SKYE TERRIER

◊ SPANIEL

◊ WHIPPET

Excerpt from *Oliver Twist* by Charles Dickens

"Give me the other," said <u>Sikes</u>, seizing <u>Oliver's</u> <u>unoccupied</u> hand. "Here, <u>Bull's-Eye</u>!"

The dog looked up, and <u>growled</u>.

"See here, boy!" said Sikes, <u>putting</u> his other hand to Oliver's throat; "if he <u>speaks</u> ever so <u>soft</u> a word, <u>hold</u> him! D'ye mind!"

The dog growled <u>again</u>; and <u>licking</u> his lips, eyed Oliver as if he were <u>anxious</u> to <u>attach</u> himself to his <u>windpipe</u> without <u>delay</u>.

"He's as <u>willing</u> as a <u>Christian</u>, <u>strike</u> me <u>blind</u> if he isn't!" said Sikes, regarding the <u>animal</u> with a kind of <u>grim</u> and <u>ferocious</u> approval. "Now, you know what you've got to <u>expect</u>, <u>master</u>, so call away as <u>quick</u> as you like; the dog will <u>soon</u> stop that <u>game</u>. Get on, young'un!"

Bull's-eye <u>wagged</u> his <u>tail</u> in acknowledgment of this unusually <u>endearing</u> <u>form</u> of <u>speech</u>; and, giving <u>vent</u> to another <u>admonitory</u> growl for the <u>benefit</u> of Oliver, led the way <u>onward</u>.

```
S O A T E Y E S L L U B A T R
M E A E O U N O C C U P I E D
T I K P A L F T N P S U T X V
L E D I E D I O I W K S F P K
I S N P S K M V R F A C O E C
C U I D C I I O E M E R S C I
K O L N E O W R N R P N D T U
I I B I R A O D T I S N E V Q
N X I W G C R L E S T O O B W
G N H G I G A I P L H O L D I
D A E O R M E E N N W S R E L
E D U I I V E N T G I O P Y L
L S M N H C A T T A A A R T I
A P A U H P U T T I N G G G N
Y N A I T S I R H C I E M A G
```

```
Y D O B D I F S O L I D L Y E
L T O E E I E R M D N J Y Y L
O D N N P L M L I I A P A C Z
E S U E O L A A A E A E D N Z
C T M R L T A M T R N O H U U
N R B G E P E Y E C G D E O M
E A E Y V R C H F G H E L B Y
G I R U E I T E Y U X M P Y L
I T M O D E R N N E L O M A I
L S E V I T C A R T G H A G M
L L E N N A H C N R U B J I A
E M R E Q U I R E S R R S L F
T T R O H S P A C E D E Y I U
N D E T E C T I O N J E P T E
I L U F T S U R T S I D Y Y A
```

Group: Working

Background: Developed from the larger Bullenbeisser breed in the late 19th century. Some of the "bull-biter" breeds' game-chasing traits remain in the modern breed.

Description: A large and solidly built breed with a short coat in a number of patterns. Its head is in proportion to its body with a large muzzle.

Temperament: Active, strong, playful, and self-assured. This is a friendly, loyal, and much-loved family dog but can be distrustful of strangers. They can channel their energy and intelligence into a number of doggy pursuits and roles from obedience and agility to therapy and drug detection roles.

Energy Level: This large dog requires a home and outdoor space to match, with plenty of exercise to burn off its ample, bouncy energy.

Scooby-Doo

```
E P V M H D E N H P A D D E E
V E N A D T A E R G F V E N E
E V L C S O R M Y S T E R Y E
L U O H G R N W A R K H F N D
M O M I I V G R H C J W M D Y
A O E N C M E O U W M R R O B
O D G E H B R Y M K U E O F O
O A M K R H G U F B E D L W O
D B T A U I D O Y W Y L E V C
Y B B R L Y K D D P O S G I S
B A L A B F O C P T H Y O N B
O Y S O S O M A W A O U B C G
O S O A S L R I G X E H E E A
C C T I N C N G L S K C A N S
S S Y Y S J Y E Y F A L T T I
```

◊ BOGEL

◊ DAPHNE BLAKE

◊ FLIM FLAM

◊ FRED JONES

◊ GREAT DANE

◊ HANNA BARBERA

◊ HOT DOG WATER

◊ MYSTERY INC.

◊ NEKARA

◊ RED HERRING

◊ RUBY-DOO

◊ RUH-ROH

◊ SCOOBY SNACKS

◊ SCOOBY-DEE

◊ SCOOBY-DOO

◊ SCOOBY-DUM

◊ SCRAPPY-DOO

◊ SHAGGY ROGERS

◊ THE HEX GIRLS

◊ THE MYSTERY MACHINE

◊ VELMA DINKLEY

◊ VINCENT VAN GHOUL

◊ WEERD

◊ YABBA-DOO

◊ CHARLIZE THERON

◊ CHRIS EVANS

◊ DAN LEVY

◊ DREW BARRYMORE

◊ EVA MENDES

◊ HILARY DUFF

◊ HILARY SWANK

◊ JANE LYNCH

◊ JON HAMM

◊ JOSH HUTCHERSON

◊ JUSTIN THEROUX

◊ KELLAN LUTZ

◊ KRISTIN BELL

◊ LIVE SCHREIBER

◊ MILEY CYRUS

◊ ORLANDO BLOOM

◊ RACHEL BILSON

◊ RYAN REYNOLDS

◊ SANDRA BULLOCK

◊ SARAH PAULSON

◊ SELENA GOMEZ

◊ SIMON COWELL

◊ TOM HARDY

◊ ZOOEY DESCHANEL

```
C D P O N D I E L E R O L T K
G F O G O D O G M A T I X F B
H W N A F K L E M I S S I S G
A P G H A L I V N O G O P W F
I D O Z L D Y I X O W C Y M G
R T A E D N E M A Y S I A D J
Y K N A F T I E M V U K R B R
M B L K S W I T U I B V T E M
A D K N T L O E M I T A T L W
C V I O R M F R C Y B T C B I
L E B A O Y A K G G I A M M G
A Y H U J O N I H N G S I U G
R C S I N A G A S L R A C J I
Y E P H D Y C J U S E N N M N
D M D O W F B K W H D W H A S
```

◊ BIG RED	◊ HUAN	◊ MOUSE
◊ CARL SAGAN	◊ JACK	◊ NELL
◊ CHARLIE	◊ JUMBLE	◊ PONGO
◊ DAISY	◊ KAZAK	◊ ROWF
◊ DOGMATIX	◊ LADDIE	◊ SNITTER
◊ EINSTEIN	◊ LORELEI	◊ TIMMY
◊ FANG	◊ MAX	◊ TOBY
◊ HAIRY MACLARY	◊ MISSIS	◊ WIGGINS

```
F S N D F P E K I N G E S E E
I O N N P E T G O N O T S O B
K U A A U I R H E F E T R S G
N E I L L O C D Y S P G E B D
O C N T C I L K E D G D X P N
L T A E B O L T E G M D O R A
L O R H G I L R O D A R B A L
I T E S S A B D G C P P R H D
P B M S M T L G H E Y A E S N
A P O O D L E S W U R E I I U
P S P R U O H D E X I M L R O
T E Y B D U C J I B I P A I F
G O L M N E L G A E B E V N W
U U T D C H R R L T M G A Y E
O W P L E I N A P S I L C G N
```

◊ BASSET HOUND

◊ BEAGLE

◊ BICHON FRISE

◊ BORDER TERRIER

◊ BOSTON TERRIER

◊ BOXER

◊ BULLDOG

◊ COCKER SPANIEL

◊ COLLIE

◊ CORGI

◊ DACHSHUND

◊ GERMAN SHEPHERD

◊ GOLDEN RETRIEVER

◊ IRISH SETTER

◊ KING CHARLES CAVALIER

◊ LABRADOR

◊ MALTESE

◊ MIXED BREED

◊ NEWFOUNDLAND

◊ PAPILLON

◊ PEKINGESE

◊ POMERANIAN

◊ POODLE

◊ PUG

◊ SHETLAND SHEEPDOG

◊ SILKY TERRIER

```
Y N A T T I R B Y M V T A B D
G V B U G R E A T D A N E S H
R Y J N D R E V E I R T E R S
E L Y S D N U H S H C A D G L
Y H S L E W A E M A L T E S E
H H C B H V T L R H I Y B P O
O C K A U T I W N H A E C T N
U P J A E L B Z G E R R E U B
N P I R W V L U S N E P E V E
D H B T S A O D E L P R F S R
W A R A B L Z S O I A E G S G
S R A E S U E A H G T K A P E
V A I G X S L W Y O A C E I R
A O P J U O E L L V R O G T E
L H K E P P B T J J C C J Z Y
```

◊ AZAWAKH

◊ BASSET
HOUND

◊ BERNESE
MOUNTAIN DOG

◊ BOXER

◊ BRITTANY

◊ COCKER
SPANIEL

◊ DACHSHUND

◊ ENGLISH
BULLDOG

◊ GOLDEN
RETRIEVER

◊ GREAT DANE

◊ GREENLAND
DOG

◊ GREYHOUND

◊ IRISH SETTER

◊ JAPANESE
SPITZ

◊ LEONBERGER

◊ MALTESE

◊ PHARAOH
HOUND

◊ PIT BULL

◊ PUG

◊ RAT TERRIER

◊ SLOUGHI

◊ VIZSLA

◊ WELSH
TERRIER

◊ WHIPPET

```
R E T E P Y Y C E C W S Y G M
L A M R I A A O L L O P P A E
L G U X C H I P S E O G F N X
N A H K N A M E L F I R G T V
H E L I H S E V R U U O B I T
C W G I A N D A E I D A S S J
N G B L E H X H T H O R N E Y
U J T A R H R S S W Y K C I R
P Y L Y D R S A U Q S S T T Q
O N U K K Y E S B A J K Z T A
J I X A T C J D O E R T I D I
E H Z U C Q U U N X K O H T G
V I A B X C X L D A L Q I O A
F E T I C H U U H Y G O E L N
B O R O S E L L E D I E S E L
```

◇ ANTIS

◇ APPOLLO

◇ BEAUTY

◇ BUSTER

◇ CHIPS

◇ DIESEL

◇ GANDER

◇ IRMA

◇ JUDY

◇ KUNO

◇ LUCCA

◇ LUCKY

◇ PETER

◇ PUNCH

◇ RICKY

◇ RIFLEMAN
    KHAN

◇ ROSELLE

◇ SADIE

◇ SALTY

◇ SASHA

◇ SHEILA

◇ THORN

◇ TICH

◇ TREO

Solutions

1

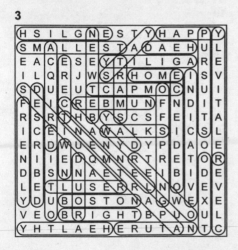

2

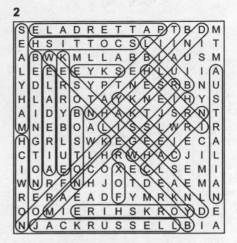

3

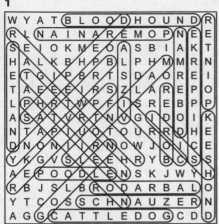

4

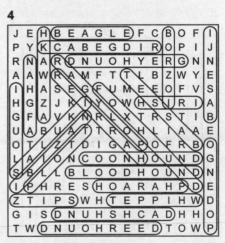

5

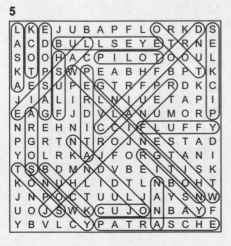

6

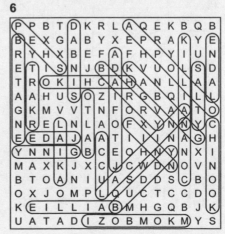

Solutions

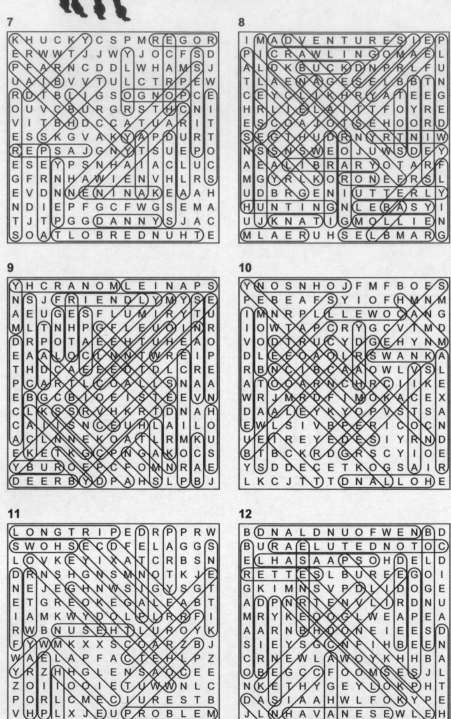

Solutions

13

```
E T U M A L A M E R O F P H R
U I P W O L F H O U N D S K E
D O E I L L O C B P D R W A Z
P Z C M E V A J M L E D G W U
G R D R A N R E B L S R O A A
R O E W A A D U T I V E E F Z N
E B A A Y H N E T E A H F A H
A R N W K Y W U N F M P I E C
T E A K I T A L O H M E T U S
D L M C T L A X B H E H S A B
A D P O G N H H U R R S A E A
N O R S D O I S O A A E M Y S
E O V F U R K A S I M C E C S
K P U N B Y T Y A R P O C D E
W P D D L C L U M B E R V O T
```

14

```
F E M O C E B C O M M O N L Y
G N E M A N A M I A B L E A A
N E P D N U O H E O M P R C I
I M U E C O F F T E U N W I A
W R R B I S I T N R S H E S L
A A P B E L E I S H A G G Y U
L W O E N R A U A P O U R H G
T N S W T L I E P L Y O A P E
U H E S M T R L R H U R L R R
O O U D R A I E U H F M D M A
B M O R R E T N L O O K I N G
R E E O D A T V P K C I H T N
E E N W W I G R E Q U I R E S
D Y L G N I S I R P R U S N U
F C U G O D E V E L O P E D J
```

15

```
T P M E T N O C D E Y A R T S
R S L P A R T I C U L A R H H
E L E M I T H T A B C E S R O
C D O T B E C O M E A D C O W
N G E V H G E R M S T E H A E
E N P V E G Y K U E B T O T V
I I E S A D I R E G S A O A E
T K E P N H E L E N P H L M R
A C P E A K E N S I N G T O N
P O I N N C I B L O V E R U O
M T N T O U L E S S O N L N I
O S G U S D A R L I N G S T S
H E G N R F S G N I T T U B S
W H E D I S E I D E M E R L A
C H I L D R E N G A G E D D P
```

16

```
G R E Y H O U N D W V N P H H
E R E Z U A N H C S A E G O O
I I F N L D E E R H O U N D A
T F L S A B G A G E O C B R R
P D I L C R I F N G N P A M A
R G R B O S A A S U E T M E H
H U I E Z C D M N A T R P D D
O A S I H T R A I E L O M R E
D F V S A P I E R E Q U L A A
E J L E E T E R D D W E K V N
S J R H A L I H L R S S A I M
I G L M U E L E S I O Z R O B
A J L Y R S N A M R E B O D G
N A Z I B I K A R I S T E T G
D D N V E G S Y T E P P I H W
```

17

```
N R E H T U O S S P S K T M I
P E L N P O V U K M H J C V D
E M M A N S S E C D S A H A T
Y I C M A S U J N L P Y L M E
A L K L O F R O N A N B D L B
F H I L A D C U I A O U T U S
C S O I R U S S I A N O L C K
H M I H O W L T S P B L V H T
I T O T N E H E L D P B I U U
E N W K Y H A N A O B Y E R R
N U E R A H I T G R S L I E N
G A K T U P O N A B U C E S S
R L K S L I S O P I A C I A Y I
I A N A S E U Q R A M Y A Y I
S L D H V E F U E G I A N A T
```

18

```
A C E T H E W O N D E R D O G
S N I G G I H I R B U D D Y O
Y F S A N G G U E N G M F H D
E S D Y R I J K N K A O N S E
D N S C G B N N R D I I R Y H
Y O M S O C N T I E T P C S T
L C C F A Y P S H N C U S O R
C B P P P O U I G T C G R E D
E V R P K N F T M E I A O G N
G S I S S U N L R U O L R O U
A K O E G I C R A Z O R L O U
S E K O R I V Y N M S A K C S
D Y N A M I T E T H E D O G T
S K E I G G U T D A I S Y I R
R K A E R T S R E V I L S K M
```

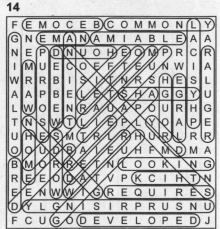
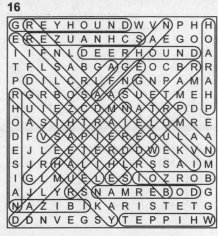
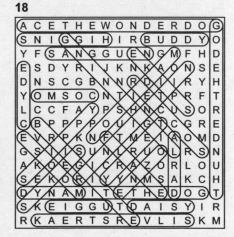
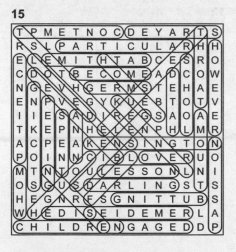
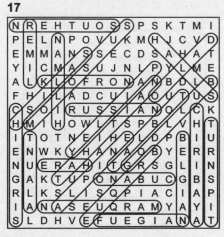

Solutions

19

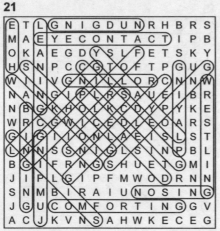

20

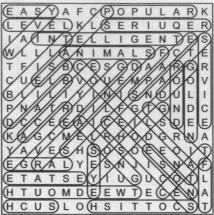

21

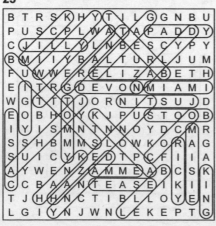

22

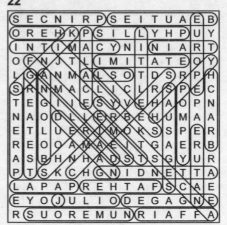

23

24

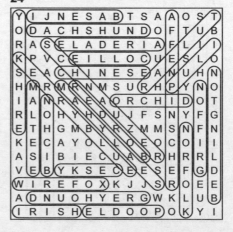

Solutions

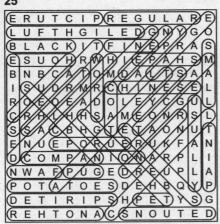

25

```
E R U T C I P  R E G U L A R E
L U F T H G I L E D  N Y G O
B L A C K  I T F I N E P R A S
E S U O H R M W H I E P A H S M
B N B C A T O M D A L T S A A
I I S U D R M R C H I N E S E L
R O E D E A D O L E C G U L
C R H L H H S A M E O N R S L
S S A C B H G T E T A O N U T
E N U E P O R U E R U K F A N
D C O M P A N I O N A R P L I
N W A F P U G E D R E U P L A
P O T A T O E S D E H B Q Y P
D E T I R I P S H P E T Y S G
R E H T O N A C S N O U T E D
```

26

```
Y T R E B I L A R A C V V G V
L U C C G N K L U C K Y V Y O
K C A J K C A L B A N C E N C
Y C J K J H R Y L N E R T N T
L J A I A T A L A C G O U L
E Y S R K N F R E C K L E S N
I Y D D U B G E I L R A H C E
L W R E B S V T O I W P L Y E
L S G A S V O K I R E I F O B
I W P D A S H R J M M K P B E
M M R O P P P A S H A S W D P
V E S J T J M H H Y J H G L A
Y O R B O R D A R N O A D O G
V R A G B W J N H E R B M E K
D A S Y E N R A B C X I K U Y
```

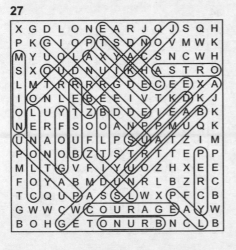

27

```
X G D L O N E A R J O J S Q H
P K G I O P T S D N O V M W K
M Y U O L A X Y A C S N C W H
S X O U D N U I K H A S T R O
L M T R R R R G D E C E E X A
I O N L E B E E I V T K D K J
O L U Y T Z B D D E I E A B K
N E R F S O O A N P P M U Q K
U N A O U F L P S U A T Z I M
P O N O B Z T S T R T T E P P
M L T G V F I Y U O Z H X E E
F O Y A B M D U N R L B Z R C
T C Q U P A S S L W X P F C B
G W W C W C O U R A G E A Y W
B O H G E T O N U R B N C L B
```

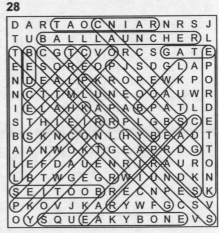

28

```
D A R T A O C N I A R N R S J
T U B A L L L A U N C H E R L
T B C G T C V O R C S G A T E
E E S O R E O P J S D G L A P
N D E A L P K R O P E W K P O
N C T T M L U N E O O A U W R
I E L A H R A P A B P A T L D
S T H I E I R R P L G B S C E
B S K N C O N L H Y B E A D T
A A N W O K T G E A P R D G T
L E F D A U E N R R A U R O
L B T W G E G R W I O N D R N
S E I T O O B R E C N P E S K
P K O V J K A R Y W F G C S V
O Y S Q U E A K Y B O N E V S
```

29

```
E N S O R Y N A G O H A M D B
G O A U M E Y N W A T I N Y R
A I D T N K D E A N R P R W O
T I I R R S L N E T I I E O U
I C G E E L H M U G U A W N G
R E N V P O L M Q S A U S H
E T I L A M R Y N H X C H R T
H O T I C Y S L X E G R O U E
K I R Y S Z P D V D L W O R G
I P H Z I E E T D E L S D E A
T N U R Y R S Y O F H S M G L
F I A X E D C O L L I E U P
E T S N H A A N L Y R U S H R
N S G C L Y L R B P O C K E T
E Y P P U P S H S H A G G Y T
```

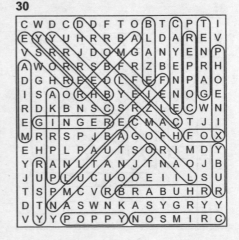

30

```
C W D C D D F T O B T C P T I
E Y Y U H R R B A L C A R E V
V S R R J D O M G A N Y E N P
A W O R R S B F R Z B E P R A H
D G H R E E D L F E F N R A O
I S A O R H B Y E I E N P E E
R D K B N S C S R Z L E C W N
M R R S P J B A G O F H F O X
E H P L P A U T S O R I M D Y
Y R A N L T A N J T N A Q J B
J U P L U C U O D E I I L S U
T S P M C V R B R A B U H R R
D T N A S W N K A S Y G R Y Y
V Y Y P O P P Y N O S M I R C
```

Solutions

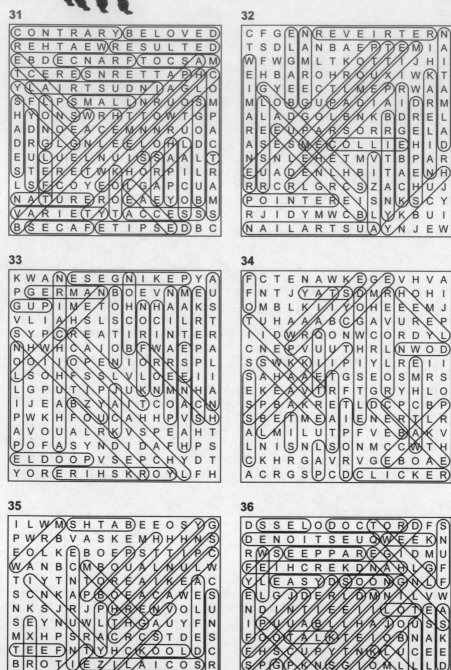

Solutions

37
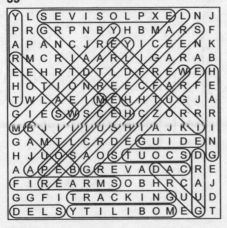

38

39
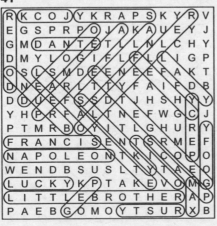

40

41

42

43

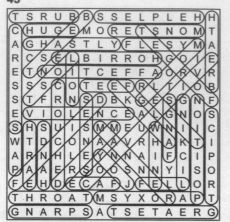

44

45

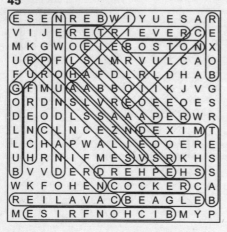

46

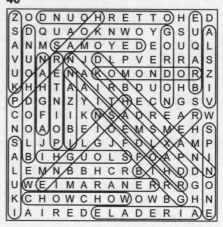

47

48

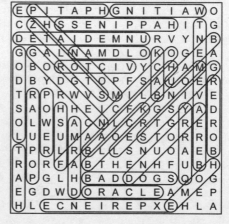

Solutions

49
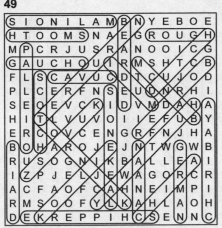

50
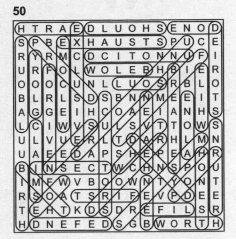

51
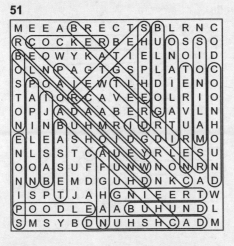

52
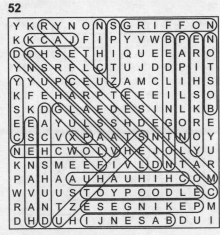

53
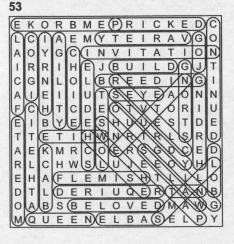

54
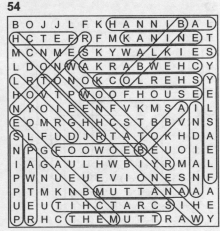

Solutions

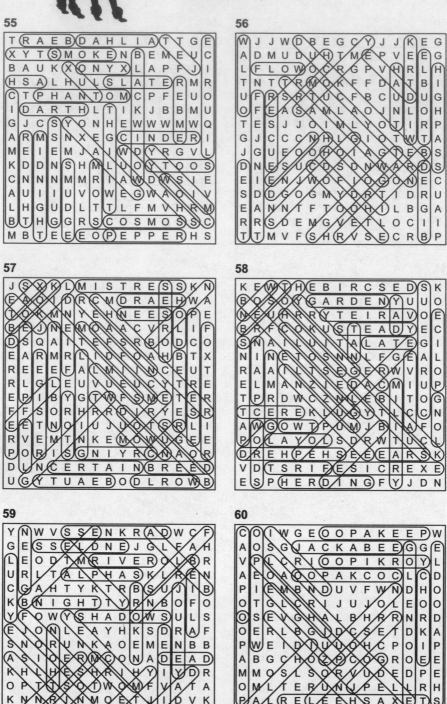

Solutions

61

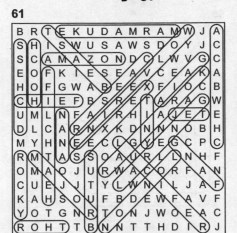

62

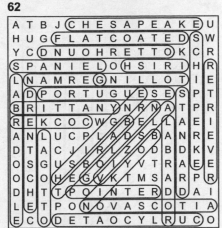

63

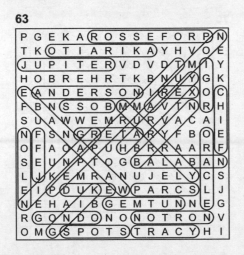

64

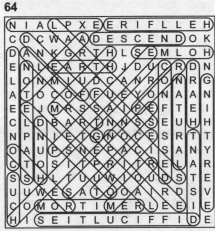

65

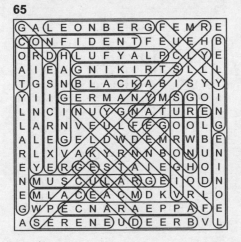

66

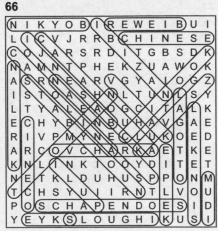

Solutions

67

```
D W I D R E I R R E T T A R W
U E H D A L M A T I A N O M E
H R X I D R E H P E H S W R I
Z P E I P Y K S U H I B G E M
S R A K M P S I U J D E N Z A
H O R R C O E T R A N Y O U R
E D P E A O Z T E C U E L A N
T A N N Q D C O D K O S L N E
L R E O O L T C R R H E I H E
A B D B T E W S O U Y N P C R
N A L D E T O A B S E I A S E
D L O E M Q O K V S R H P U T
U J G R H N Q E E G C S S Z
E I P L E K J M A L I N O I S
I T V I Z S L A P L M M N E H
```

68

```
L O D N A L D N U O H W E N L
I Y T W D O G O M I T E S G W
C H W W P S M O R Y S T A U O
K W A Y A A G I U S D I O U O
T D P E A P R U A A N S A H S
E G A L B R A H D A I B D S T
N V G E C E A M B V A T A I E
S K N K A L I L A R O P N D R
T P I R I T W A K N A B E A P
E U S A E O A C R W I B R G E
I P T B H Y E B T U R K R O E
N U N K C L A U A D F D R D
M A I L O R G N O M E F G A D
T P N N K A Y A R A B K R A B
B F A U L H O U N D U R A S O
```

69

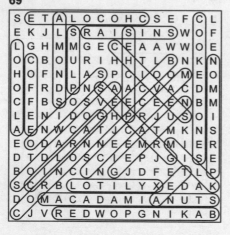

```
S E T A L O C O H C S E F C L
E K J L S R A I S I N S W O F
L G H M M G E C E A A W W O E
O C B O U R I H H T L B N K N
H O F N L A S P C I O O M E O
O C F R D P N S A A C V A C D M
C F B S O S V E E C E E N B M
L E N I D O G H P R J U S O I
A E N W C A T J C A T M K N S
E O D A R N N E E M R M I E R
D T D L O S C I E P J G I S E
B O I N C I N G J D F E T L P
S C R B L O T I L Y X E D A K
D O M A C A D A M I A N U T S
C J V R E D W O P G N I K A B
```

70

```
T G L B C I T S E M O D H T M
T N E T R W S A B E E E R V E
E I K N S O E G M C R R E V R D
X K G O S I E N E D L I E E I
T R T M L N E D I A S C S S U
U O H I T I I N H R T T D E M
R W T A D S G B E S H E N R D
E Y L E N R E G N O L X E V I
S B B O P T N R U L U C R E G
I O C U T A E G I S H E D D O
C R P E R T H F O V A L L K R
R D R T T Y L I M A F S I A O
E S A O U T S I D E H H A U
X R P C F E R E S R A O C T U
E N E R G E T I C H T O O M S
```

71

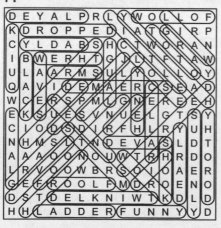

```
D E Y A L P R L Y W O L L O F
K D R O P P E D I A T G I R P
C Y L D A B S H C T W O R A N
I B W E R H T G J L T F T A W
U L A A R M S U L Y O L L O Y
Q A V I D E M A E R C S E A D
W C E R S P M L G N E R E E H
E K S U E S V N U E L G T S Y
C I O D S D I R F H L R Y U H
N H M S D T N D E V A S L D T
A A A O N O U W T R H R D O R
L R V O O W B R S O I O A E N
G E F R O O L F M D R Q E N O
D S T D E L K N I W T K D L D
H H L A D D E R F U N N Y Y D
```

72

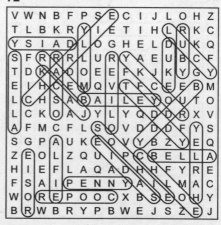

```
V W N B F P S E C I J L O H Z
T L B K R Y I E T I H L R K C
Y S I A D L O G H E L D U K Q
S F R R R L U R Y A E U B C F
T D K A O E E F K J K Y G Y
E I H C E M Q V T F C E E B M
L L C H S A B A I L E Y O U T O
L A C K O A J Y L Y Q D D R X V
A F M C F L S Q V D D D F Y S
S G P A U K E O V Y B Z Y E Q
Z E O L Z Q U I P C B E L L A
H I E F L A Q A D H H F Y R E
F S A I P E N N Y A I L M A C
W O R E P O O C X B S E O H Y
B R W B R Y P B W E J S Z E J
```

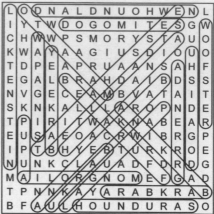

Solutions

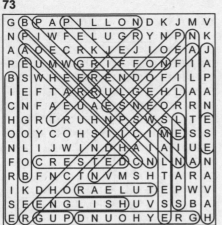

73

74

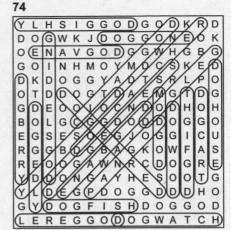

75

76

77

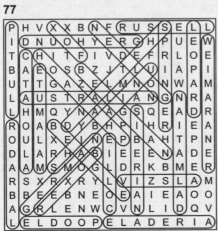

78

Solutions

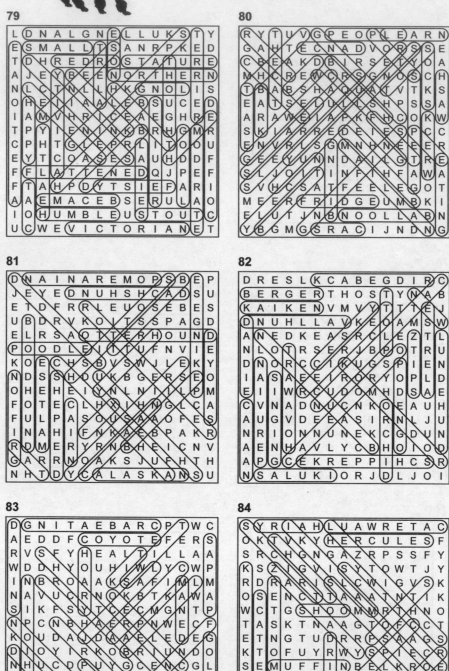

79

80

81

82

83

84

Solutions

85

86

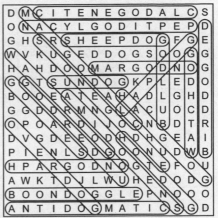

87

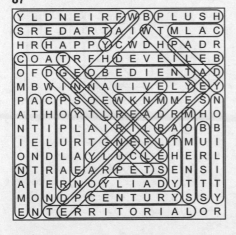

88

89

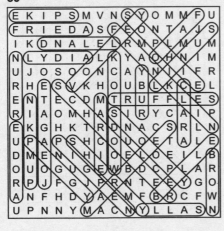

90

Solutions

91

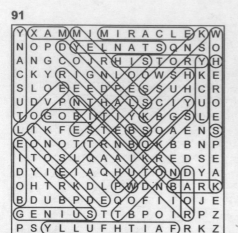

92

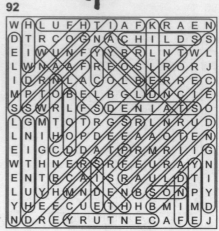

93

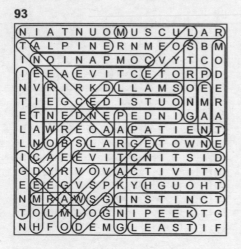

94

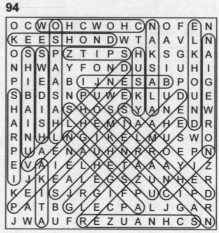

95

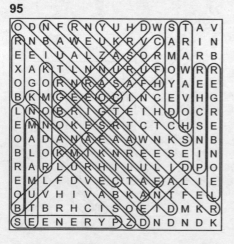

96

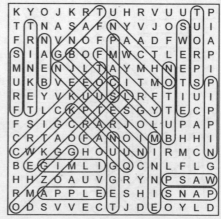

Solutions

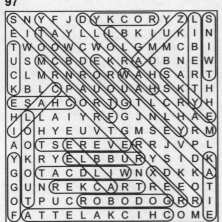

97

98

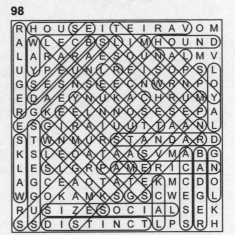

99

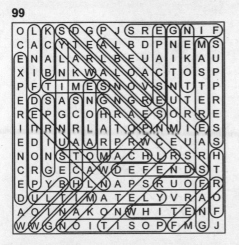

100

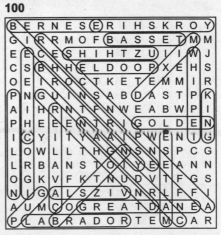

101

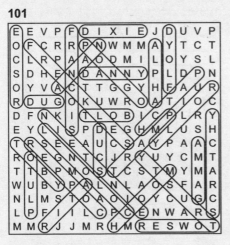

102

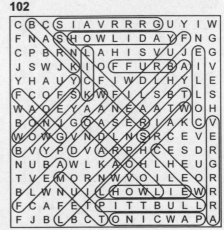

Solutions

103

104

105

106

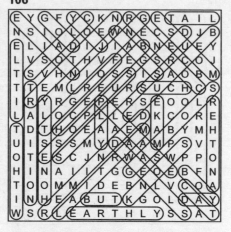

107

108

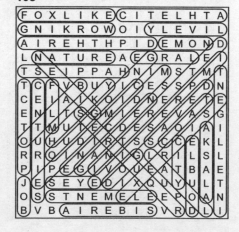

Solutions

109

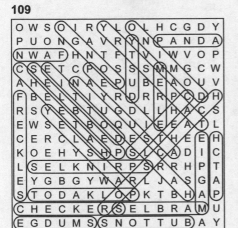

110

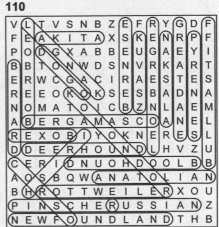

111

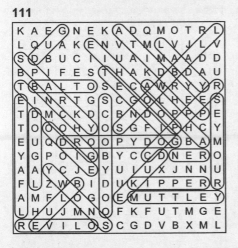

112

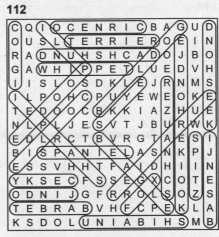

113

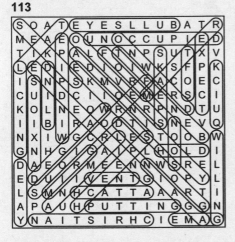

114

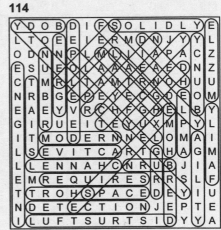

Solutions

115

116

117

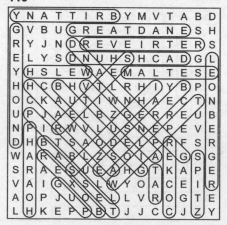

118

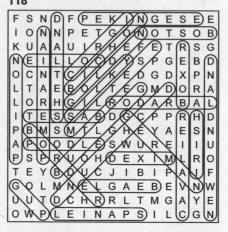

119

120

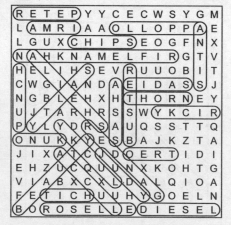